The Gates of New Life

The Gates of New Life

BY

JAMES S. STEWART, D.D.

'Would I suffer for him that I love? So wouldst Thou—so wilt Thou! ..
''Tis the weakness in strength, that I cry for! my flesh, that I seek
In the Godhead! I seek and I find it. O Saul, it shall be
A Face like my face that receives thee; a Man like to me,
Thou shalt love and be loved by, for ever: a Hand like this hand
Shall throw open the gates of new life to thee! See the Christ stand!'
David, in BROWNING's Saul.

HODDER AND STOUGHTON
LONDON SYDNEY AUCKLAND TORONTO

TO

THE CONGREGATIONS OF

ST. ANDREW'S, AUCHTERARDER

BEECHGROVE, ABERDEEN

AND

NORTH MORNINGSIDE, EDINBURGH

WITH GRATITUDE AND AFFECTION

'I thank my God upon every remembrance of you.'

Acknowledgments

A few of these studies have already appeared in print; and for permission to include them here I am grateful to the editors and publishers of *The Expository Times*, *The Speaker's Bible*, *St. Martin's Review*, *The British Weekly*, *The Home Messenger*, *Modern Sermons* (Faber & Faber), and *The Christian Faith To-Day* (Student Christian Movement).

Contents

I

Clouds and Darkness and the Morning Star

> 'If one look unto the land, behold darkness and
> sorrow and the light is darkened in the heavens thereof.'
> Isa. v, 30.

> 'I am the bright and morning star.' — Rev. xxii. 16.

OF ALL THE DOUBTS WHICH, AS BROWNING PUTS IT, CAN 'RAP
and knock and enter in our soul', by far the most devastating
is doubt of the ultimate purpose of God. You may doubt
some of the dogmas of your ancestors, and be none the worse
for it. You may doubt a particular article in a credal state-
ment, and still be on the Lord's side. You may doubt the
validity of contemporary fashions in religious thinking, and
still have your feet upon the Rock of Ages. But to doubt
the final purpose of God — which means to doubt the
rationality of the universe, and significance of human experience, and the worth of moral values — is there anything
left to live for then?

Yet what is precisely the doubt which is lying like an
appalling weight on multitudes of lives today. They would
think twice before subscribing to Tennyson's faith:

'Yet I doubt not thro' the ages one increasing purpose
    runs,
And the thoughts of men are widen'd with the process of
    the suns.'

'Where is any evidence of such a purpose?' they want to

ask. 'Where is any convincing trace of plan or pattern or design? It does not make sense — this tangled world. We are not getting anywhere. We are just blundering along, victims of fate and chance and accident; and all our dreams and hopes and idealisms and struggles are a mere forlorn futility.'

So they are back where Ecclesiastes was. 'Vanity of vanities, all is vanity.' What is the use, cried Thomas Hardy, of all your prayers, you praying people, when you have nothing better to pray to than

'The dreaming, dark, dumb Thing
That turns the handle of this idle Show?'

'A bad joke' — that was Voltaire's final verdict on life. 'Ring down the curtain,' said the dying actor, 'the farce is done.'

People do not go about saying these things, of course. Not in so many words. But deep down in the hidden recesses of many a soul that doubt has begun to stir. Has God a plan?

Mark you, they are not flippant souls whom that doubt afflicts. Some of the most lovable and devoted people in the world are in the toils of it today. There was a man I knew: he turned in, with this particular burden on his heart, to a church one day. The preacher's sermon was a hotch-potch of Emersonian optimism, plus a dash of Coué: the world was getting better and better every day, and everything in the garden of the human heart was lovely, and soon we should all reach the New Jerusalem by our own momentum. That man left the church that day not only hurt, but angry. I don't blame him. I think it would have angered Christ. Face the facts! That is Christ's first rule of honesty. And when men do sincerely endeavour to face the facts, do you think it is so very surprising that sometimes a doubt of the ultimate meaning of it all creeps in? Read your Isaiah. He might have been writing for today. 'If one look unto the land, behold darkness and sorrow, and the light is darkened in the heavens thereof.'

Now this doubt of an ultimate plan or purpose in life springs from various sources; and I am going to ask you at this point to imagine that we have here in the church two or three typical representatives, who are going to speak for themselves.

Here is one. 'My doubt of an ultimate purpose in things,' he tells us, 'comes from science.' 'Will you explain?' we ask him. 'Well, it is like this,' he goes on. 'It is now a recognised fact that the universe we inhabit is gradually — very slowly, but none the less certainly — running down like a clock, with its energy imperceptibly but steadily degenerating. And if that is true, if that is the line of our destiny, is there any sense in talking of an ultimate purpose or a plan?' Now it is a real difficulty; and even if I were to point out to this speaker that a universe which is running down like a clock must first have been wound up by some one, and that therefore his own argument points to a divine mind in control; even if I were to remind him that in any case Christianity never suggested that our home here was permanent ('The world passeth away'), it is hardly likely that this would dispel his doubt. Some better answer will be required. There is a better answer. There is, in Christianity, an overwhelmingly convincing answer. We are coming to that soon. Meanwhile, the difficulty stands.

Take a second man. 'It is not science,' he tells us, 'that has led me to doubt the purpose of God: it is the state of the world. It is this pitiless, unending struggle for existence among the nations. It is the collapse of our idealisms before the brute facts of force and chaos. It is the feeling that there is something demonic in the heart of things which is working against us, that there is a radical twist in the very constitution of the universe which will always defeat man's hopes, make havoc of his dreams, and bring his pathetic optimism crashing in disaster. Purpose? Look at the world! That settles it.'

Take a third man. 'It is neither science nor history,' he tells us, 'that has shaken my faith in a divine plan. It is the fact of suffering.' And then perhaps he quotes the words of the philosopher Hume. 'Were a stranger to drop suddenly into this world, I would show him, as a specimen of its ills, a hospital full of diseases, a prison crowded with malefactors and debtors, a field of battle strewn with carcases, a fleet floundering in the ocean, a nation languishing under tyranny, famine, or pestilence.' 'Honestly,' he declares, 'I don't see how you can possibly square that with an ultimate purpose of love.' And indeed, I wonder if any one here has never felt, like cold steel running into his soul, the sudden stab of that wild doubt? There is a most poignant moment in Eugene O'Neill's play, *All God's Chillun got Wings*. 'Will God forgive me?' one of the characters asks another. And the answer comes — 'Maybe He can forgive what you've done to me; and maybe He can forgive what I've done to you; but I don't see how He's going to forgive — Himself.' It is the same haunting doubt. Is there any loving purpose in command?

We have imagined these three men speaking frankly of their problem — one arguing from science, another from the condition of the world, a third from the mystery of suffering. But perhaps for someone here the problem is more intimate and personal still. It is not really science, nor the world, nor an abstract problem of evil that is your worry. It is your own experience. The psalmist advised us, when the low mood came, to address our own souls, and say, 'Why art thou cast down, O my soul?' But there are multitudes of people who know perfectly well what their souls would answer.

'Cast down? How can I help it? Life has been so different

from what I had hoped, so full of thwarting and frustration; and I seem to be of so little use to anyone, and if I died to-night the world would go on tomorrow as if nothing at all had happened. And this struggle to achieve something like a decent character — what a weary business that has been! This troublesome self — ten years, twenty years ago, I was fighting that; and here I am, fighting the same thing still. And what's the use? I feel so tragically ineffective and futile. Don't talk to me of a divine purpose in my life! For that I can't believe.'

We have listened, then, to these different voices; and I think you will realise that what they are doing is to force us up against the most crucial alternative, the most inescapable 'Either-Or' of life. That alternative is this: Either despair — or faith. Either blank, unrelieved pessimism, or a gambler's throw with your soul. Either darkness and futility and ulti-mate night, or the vision of God standing within the shadow, keeping watch above His own.

There is no third way. It is between these two readings of life that every soul of us must choose. But it is precisely here that Christianity comes in with its central demand. It demands that, before we choose, we should at least try to see what the men of the New Testament had seen.

What was that? They had seen one point of light in the darkness. They had wrestled desperately with this strange puzzle of life, its problems and griefs and breaking hearts; and then God had put into their hands one word, and they looked at it, and suddenly they realized that this was the solving word, the code word, and that they had only to apply this to decipher all the rest. They had pored long on life's jumbled, meaningless pieces, trying vainly to make sense of them; and then one day the semblance of a pattern had ap-peared, not much of a design, it is true, just two lines like a cross — but at least it was a pattern; and with this standing out, somehow all the other things began to move into their place. In the maze of life's perplexities, they had come upon one fact that made the idea of a blessed purpose suddenly credible. They — the common soldiers on life's field — had been allowed for one moment to glimpse the great Commander-in-Chief's plan of campaign. In one flash across the darkness they had caught a sight of God's meaning with the universe and with themselves. They had seen Jesus.

And this stands today as the central demand of Christianity, that when you and I are baffled by life and cannot see purpose in it anywhere, and when we stand facing the final alternative of despair or faith, we should not decide until we have included the fact of Jesus in our evidence, and taken cognizance of His life and death and victory, and seen across the midnight darkness that bright and morning star.

This, of course, is not to exclude the possibility of other evidence. Go to Nature, for example. Is there no trace of purpose there? Have not scientists like Jeans and Eddington been telling us that everything points to the existence of an infinite, directing mind, as of a great mathematician? Does not the vast system of ordered natural law imply that ultimately the universe itself is on the side of righteousness — which is what the Bible means when it says, 'the stars in their courses fought against Sisera'? And is there not a deeper meaning than some of us have suspected in the words of a familiar hymn?

'But the slow watches of the night
  Not less to God belong;
And for the everlasting right
  The silent stars are strong.'

Or turn to History. Is there no trace of purpose there? Erratic and incalculable the course of events may often be; but do no clear principles stand out? This at least has surely emerged from the long travail of the ages, that 'where there is no vision, the people perish,' and that where there is moral apostasy, there comes inevitably national decay. Does that not indicate purpose?

Or turn to your own experience. 'I came about,' said Robert Louis Stevenson, describing a decisive stage of his soul's career, 'like a well-handled ship. There stood at the wheel that unknown steersman whom we call God.' Perhaps there has been no such dramatic hand of Providence in your experience. But before you deny the presence of an over-ruling purpose, think again! I put this to you now: Are there not certain things you would die rather than do? Are there not certain ideals of honour and truth that have an absolute claim on you, so that you can only say, 'Here stand I: I and no other'? Where does that feeling come from? Do you really believe Bertrand Russell when he asserts that it is just 'the outcome of accidental collocation of atoms'? Were the heroisms of the martyrs, and the preaching of a Savonarola, and the devotion of a Wilberforce, and the sacrifice of a Livingstone, and the shudder that passed over your own soul when the first real temptation came, and the peace that followed when you conquered — were these things the product of chance groupings of atoms? Do you not think that that explanation is definitely less plausible, far more incredible, than the Christian one, according to which that sense of honour, that resolve to die rather than do certain things, is the grip of a living God upon your soul; in other words, the clear token of a great purpose working through your life?

Yes, there are these lines of evidence. God has not left himself without a witness to His purpose in nature, history, experience. But that is not enough. Men never felt that it was enough. Still the mists of uncertainty linger. Still the shadows of the dread doubt darken the soul. But suddenly, out of the mists comes Jesus! High in the darkened heavens rides a messenger of hope. I am the bright and morning star!

How do I know, looking at Jesus, that life has a meaning, and God a purpose! *I know it from His character*. Into this tumbled, chaotic world there has appeared at one point of time that quality of life — absolute chivalry, consistency unwavering, love triumphant over every evil, compassion as wide as the sea, purity as steady as a rock. And when I gaze at that, immediately there is a voice in my own heart that begins to cry — 'The meaning of life is there! God's purpose for me, and for all humanity, is there. Soul of mine, follow the gleam!'

How do I know, looking at Jesus, that life has a meaning, and God a purpose? *I know it from His cross*. When a flag is flying in the wind, you cannot always make out its design and pattern; but then perhaps there comes a sudden stormy gust, and blows the flag out taut, and for a moment the pattern stands out clear. Was it not something like that which happened over nineteen hundred years ago? The flag of life and of man's long campaign had been flying for ages, and none could read its meaning; but suddenly came a storm-blast, the fiercest gust of all, and straightened out the flag: and men looked, and lo! its pattern was a cross. Does it not help you, in your own sufferings, to know that that cross is the ground-plan of the universe, that life is built like that; that the trials and troubles and sacrifices which often seem so meaningless, the very negation of all purpose, are really the means by which the most glorious purpose imaginable is being wrought out; and that therefore every pain you have to bear can be a holy sacrament in which the God who suffered on Calvary comes to meet you, and your contribution to the building of the kingdom of heaven and the redeeming of the world? Christ died to tell us that.

How do I know, looking at Jesus, that life has a meaning, and God a purpose? *I know it from His resurrection*. Do you remember the dramatic passage in which Browning likens conversion to the effect of a lightning-flash in a dark night, showing up everything momentarily as clear as day?

'I stood at Naples once, a night so dark
I could have scarce conjectured there was earth
Anywhere, sky or sea or world at all:
But the night's black was burst through by a blaze . . .
There lay the city thick and plain with spires,
And, like a ghost disshrouded, white the sea.
So may the truth be flashed out by one blow.'

What was the resurrection of Jesus? What were the appearances to the disciples? They were the lightning-flash of God, the bursting of the unseen world into the seen, the break through of God's new creation, the spiritual world order, into the order that now is. No wonder Paul, meeting Jesus outside the gates of Damascus, fell blinded to the earth! What had he seen? Do not think it was the Syrian sunshine that dazzled him. No! He had seen — for one tremendous moment, in that risen, death-defeating Christ, he had seen — the unveiled purpose of God. And you who have been where Paul and these disciples were, you who on some high road of the spirit have met the risen Christ again and felt the thrill and glory of His power, you to whom He is now the companion of the way in a blessed intimacy of friendship whose wonders never cease — you need no further proof. Life does have a meaning and a purpose and a goal. And we poor struggling creatures are not the doomed playthings of chance and accident and futility. We are getting somewhere. We are moving onwards to a day when this suffering, tormented creation shall see at last of the travail of its soul, and this corruptible shall put on incorruption, and this mortal shall put on immortality, and God shall be all in all.

'I am the bright and morning star,' says Jesus. It all comes back in the end to the question: Who will follow that gleam? Are we prepared to live now as those who have seen the purpose of God, as men and women who have tasted the powers of the world to come? And will we hold to it in spite of everything, in spite of the tangles and the darkness and all our own secret sorrows and disappointments and defeats, that God's will is coming out at the last; that though hindered often and set back by human blindness and folly and sin, its ultimate victory is sure? O trust that morning Star! God set it in the sky for you.

> 'And all the jarring notes of life
>   Seem blending in a psalm,
> And all the angles of its strife
>   Slow rounding into calm.
>
> And so the shadows fall apart,
>   And so the west winds play;
> And all the windows of my heart
>   I open to the day.'

II

The Lord God Omnipotent Reigneth

'Alleluia: for the Lord God omnipotent reigneth.' —
REV. xix. 6.

WHAT IS THE BIGGEST FACT IN LIFE TO YOU AT THIS MOMENT?
What is the real centre of your universe? 'The biggest fact in
life?' replies one man. 'Well, I reckon it is my home. That,
for me, is the centre of everything.' A very noble thing to
be able to say! 'The main fact in life to me,' says a second, 'is,
without any shadow of doubt, my work. If you take that
away from me, you take just everything.' 'The central thing
for me,' declares a third, 'is health and happiness. As long
as I have that, I am quite content. I can't bear to be unhappy.' But what is your own answer?

I know what Jesus' answer was. Was it home? No —
though none has ever hallowed home-life as Jesus hallowed
it. Work, then? No — though none has toiled so terribly as
the Son of God. Health and happiness? No — though none
has been responsible for nearly so much clean happiness and
mental and physical health as Jesus. The central fact in life
to Jesus was none of these things. It was this — 'the Lord
God omnipotent reigneth!'

Is that your answer? More blessed than home, unspeak-
ably blessed as home may be; more crucial than work, be
that work never so urgent; more vital than health and
happiness, though sometimes, especially when you lose
them, happiness and health seem to be the only things
that matter — greater and higher and deeper and more

paramount than them all — the fact of God! The power behind every thought of your brain and every beat of your heart and every breath of your body — God! The element in which you live and move and have your being — God! The final, irreducible, and inescapable denominator of your universe — God! That was the conviction on which Christ staked His life and marched to Calvary; that is the conviction which has inspired the breed of the saints; and that is the conviction which can turn very ordinary people like ourselves into men and women of whom Christ and the saints will not need to be ashamed; this conviction, strong as steel, firm as a rock, and stirring as a battle-cry: 'The Lord God omnipotent reigneth!'

Now that cardinal conviction will be found, when you explore and examine it, to lead to three results. It involves three tremendous consequences, and as these concern us all most intimately, I would ask you to think of them now.

It means, first, *the liberation of life*. It means a sense of absolute release. Release from what?

Release from petty worries, to begin with. Every one knows how sometimes things which are comparatively unimportant can obsess the mind and blot out all the sunshine. Here, let us say, is a man to whom some slight or some injustice has been administered, and he cannot get it out of his mind; he has not the grace to perform a surgical operation on that rankling thing, to cut it out and eradicate it; but he keeps on brooding and brooding about it, with his mind continually coming back to it, and going round it in wearisome circles — until the last vestige of peace of soul has been destroyed, his whole outlook on life warped, and all his sky obliterated by the mists and murky fogs of what is, from any spiritual standpoint, a wretched, insignificant triviality. Run and tell him, 'The Lord God omnipotent reigneth!' Tell him to bring his worry into the light of that great truth, and just see how the fretting thing will fade and die. This, mark you, is not fancy nor hyperbole: it is proved experience, and the grace of the Lord Jesus Christ is in it.

The fact of the matter is, as Robert Browning said succinctly, ' 'Tis looking downward that makes one dizzy.' The man who has his gaze riveted on the narrow little circle of his own experience, obsessed (like the poor creature in Bunyan's dream) with the sticks and straws and dust of the floor, never thinking of the stars and the crown, cannot see life in true perspective. Oh, if only he would look away from all that — one long look into the face of the Lord God Almighty, if only he would take even five minutes in the morning to stabilise his soul by remembering Christ, how that would reinforce and liberate him! Yes, it is release — this great conviction — from the worries of life.

Notice, further, that it means release from the fears of life, and especially from the fear of tasks that seem too great for us. Life is forever trying to make us lose our nerve and turn away from new responsibilities, saying like Jeremiah, 'I can't do this! You must let me off: I am not the man for it. Please, God, get someone else!' Do you know what it means, when you have some particularly difficult duty confronting you, to lie awake through the night, revolving your anxious fears? You have that dreadful three-o'clock-in-the-morning feeling, 'I'll never get through this! I'll never be able for it.' But if religion cannot help us there, there is something wrong.

I remember Dr. John Mott telling some of us of a conversation which he had had with Dr. Cheng, the great Christian leader in China. 'Would it not be a great thing,' said Dr. Cheng, 'for all of us Christians in China to unite, and go out and double the number of Protestant Church Christians within the next five years?' Dr. Mott asked, 'How many are there now?' 'Four hundred and thirty-five thousand,' was the answer. 'Well,' said Dr. Mott, 'it has taken over a hundred years to build in China a Christian Church of these dimensions, and do you now suggest the practicability of doubling that number in five years?' And Mott said that never would he forget the answer. 'Why not?' exclaimed that gallant Chinese leader. 'Why not?' and indeed, when a man has seen God — *why not?* 'Impossible?' cried Richard Cobden when they had been criticising as wild and fanciful and quite unfeasible his agitation for the repeal of the Corn Laws, 'Impossible? If that is all that is the matter, I move we go ahead!' And again — why not, if 'the Lord God omnipotent reigneth'? It is release from the fears of life.

Moreover, it is release from self-contempt. One fact which modern psychology has been driving home to our minds is this, that there are multitudes of people today who are losing half the happiness which God intended them to have, and are being made quite unnecessarily miserable by inward repressions and conflicts and self-contemnings with which they do not know how to deal. And all the time there lies in religion (I am thinking, mark you, not of religion of the unbalanced, over-emotional, unduly introspective type, for that may easily do more harm than good, but of the sane healthy, objective religion of Jesus of Nazareth) the power to end the conflict and to set the prisoned soul free. What is the key with which Christ's religion unlocks the prison door? What but this, 'The Lord God omnipotent reigneth'? 'There,' declares Jesus, 'is the Father of whom you — even you — are a son. Son of man, stand upon your feet! Son of the omnipotent God, lift up your head and be free!'

Release from worry, release from fear, release from self-contempt — all that is bound up with this great central conviction of the faith. It means the liberation of life.

But that is not all. Notice now, in the second place, that it means *the doom of sin*. It proclaims the ultimate defeat of evil in every shape and form.

Take this book of Revelation. You know the historic background of the book. It is a background of blood and smoke and martyrdom and reckless cynical laughter. Here you have the Rome of the Caesars and the Church of the Galilean locked in the death-grapple. Here you have the mailed fist of Nero and Domitian smashing its way through the hopes and dreams of the saints. Here you have, in the words of an old psalmist, 'the kings of the earth taking counsel together against the Lord, and against His Anointed, saying, "Let us break their bands asunder, and cast away their cords from us!"' Here you have the second Babylon, mother of all the abominations of the earth, drunk with the blood of the friends of Jesus, laughing in the intoxication of her triumph, shrieking with laughter to see the poor, pathetic Body of Christ being crushed and mangled and battered out of existence. That is the background when this man takes up his pen to write. And you and I look over his shoulder, wonder what his message is going to be. What can it be, we think, but an elegy and a lament? 'The battle is lost! Our cause is ruined. There is nothing left but to sue for mercy.' Is that what we see him writing? No! But this — flinging defiance at all the facts, and with the ring of iron in it and the shout of the saints behind it — 'Hallelujah! Babylon is fallen, is fallen!' And why? What made the man write like that? It was because at the back of the visible world, at the back of Caesar and all his pomp and pride, he had seen something which Caesar never saw, something which spelt the doom of Caesar and of all sin like Caesar's for ever: a throne upreared above the earth, and on the throne the Lord God omnipotent reigning!

We sometimes talk pessimistically about the future of Christianity. We find ourselves wondering what will be the ultimate issue in the warfare between good and evil. Is it not possible that force and injustice may prevail, and that the Jesus whom we love may go down at last before powers that are too strong for Him? But to anyone who has seen what this writer of Revelation saw, that is no longer an open question. Evil is done for — already. 'Well,' someone may say incredulously, 'it certainly does not look like it. Look at the international scene. Look at our current literature. Look at the chaos in morals. See how evil flaunts itself in the open, how it strikes its roots deeper and still deeper.' Yes, I know. But I know also this, that if God is on the throne of the universe, then evil is doomed, never has been anything else but doomed, doomed from the foundation of the world!

Now no one was ever so sure of this as Jesus. There was a day when the seventy followers whom He had sent out into the surrounding villages to preach and to heal returned to him, with their faces eager and glowing and triumphant. 'Master,' they cried excitedly, 'Master, it works — this new power that has been given to us — it really works! We have proved it. The darkest, foulest, most stubborn spirits are subject to us through Thy name!' Whereupon, says the evangelist, Jesus, hearing that glad news, and realising its deeper significance, which even they could not quite fathom, had a sudden vision. 'I beheld Satan,' He exclaimed, 'as lightning fall from heaven!' as though to say — 'This message which you have brought settles and confirms and ratifies My hope. The power of darkness is broken, snapped, done for; and henceforth the initiative is with God!'

Or take the amazing scene which meets you at the end. Have you not gazed in wonder at the sight of Christ before His judges? How calm and self-possessed He was, far more self-possessed than Caiaphas, or Pilate, or Herod, or any of the other actors on that tragic stage! What was the secret of it? Was it just His innate heroism asserting itself? Was it just Christ's way of steeling His heart to be brave? Was it only a reckless contempt of death? No. It was the open vision that behind Caiaphas, and behind Pilate, and behind

Herod, there was Someone else; and that it was not they nor any earthly governor who reigned in Jerusalem that night, but that Other, that watching, brooding Figure among the shadows — God! And Caiaphas, Pilate, Herod — who or what were they? Less than the dust beneath time's chariot-wheels. The Lord God omnipotent reigneth!

Such was the source of Jesus' heroism. And such, in the face of all the evils of the world, has been the source of the blessed optimism of the saints in every age. God is on the throne: therefore evil is doomed. 'Here on this Rock,' said Jesus once, 'I will build my Church, and the gates of hell shall not prevail against it.' Here on the Rock! That sudden cry of Christ, echoing down into the world of darkness, must have shaken that world to its foundations — like the thunderous chant of a great marching host, fair as the moon, clear as the sun, terrible as an army with banners. Francis Xavier, four hundred years ago, said a magnificent thing about the Christian mission to the Far East. 'You may be very sure of one thing,' he declared, 'the devil will be tremendously sorry to see the Company of the Name of Jesus enter China.' And then he went on — 'Just imagine! A thing so vile as I am to bring down such a vast reputation as the devil's! What great glory to God!' Do you ask what is the mainspring of Christian hope and courage? It is the certainty that we are not fighting a losing battle; that evil, flaunt itself as it may, carries the seal of its own doom upon it; and that the real pull of the universe is on the side of the man who goes out for righteousness.

Fight on, then, you who have lost heart because your own conflict is so difficult, your tempter so strong and dogged and subtle. Fight on! It is your battle, not his. For the Lord God omnipotent reigneth.

We have seen, then, two decisive consequences bound up with our text: the liberation of life, and the doom of sin. I ask you, finally, to observe that we have here *the comfort of sorrow*.

The man who wrote the twenty-ninth psalm, which we were reading today, had a marvellous sense of the dramatic. Do you remember how he sums up the great old story of the Flood in Genesis? He is looking back across the ages, and in imagination he can see that horror of the encroaching waters, rolling their waves higher and still higher, creeping up with slow, inexorable destruction and death, beating down all fragile human defences built against them — until men and women, staring at those mounting waters, felt terror clutching at their throats, for the end of the world seemed nigh. All that, the psalmist sees; but he sees something else as well. 'The Lord,' he cries, 'sat as King at the Flood,' Then, like a great shout — 'Yea, the Lord sitteth King for ever!'

And what of the floods of life? What shall we say of the days which every soul must know when, as Jesus put it, 'the rain descends, and the floods come, and the winds blow and beat upon the house,' until your whole structure of things, all your philosophy of life, is threatening to come toppling down? What about the happinesses you build for yourself — the plans you lay, the dreams you dream, the hopes you cherish, and the heart's desires you yearn for — and then, thundering and rolling mountain-high come the waves and the breakers, crashing down on that shore of dreams, leaving only some poor bits of wreckage behind? What then? Why then, blessed be God, the Lord sits as King at the flood, the Lord sitteth King for ever! Which simply means that the heartbreaking things of life have meaning and purpose and grace in them, for the Lord God omnipotent reigneth.

There was a terrible night out on the Galilean Lake when the sudden whirlwind blew, and the sea was lashed to fury and the boat struggled in the troughs of the waves, and the disciples were telling themselves — 'Our last hour has come:

this is the end!' And there was Jesus, sleeping through it all. 'Master, Master, carest Thou not that we perish?' But that night they learned by the grace of God this lesson — that there is something higher in human experience than life's waves and storms: there is a Christ who rules the waves! Have we discovered that? It is a great thing, when the floods begin and the desolation of sorrow comes beating down, to hear the divine *sursum corda* — up with your heart! — for the Lord sits King at the flood, your flood, and the Lord God omnipotent reigneth!

Did not Chesterton, in one of his most vivid poems, preach the same victory of the soul?

> 'Though giant rains put out the sun,
>   Here stand I for a sign.
> Though Earth be filled with waters dark,
>   My cup is filled with wine.
> Tell to the trembling priests that here
>   Under the deluge rod,
> One nameless, tattered, broken man
>   Stood up and drank to God.'

There was once a flood called Calvary. And all the bitterness and ugliness, all the shame and sorrow of life, entered into that flood, and came beating around the brave soul of Jesus, sweeping Him down at last to the barbarity and infamy of the death of the cross. 'What can God have been doing?' we want to ask. 'Was He asleep? Or on a journey? Or was He dead?' No! The Lord was sitting as King at the flood, that surging flood of Calvary; and out of that grim cross He has brought the salvation of the world. Tell me — if God did that with the cross of Jesus, do you think your cross can be too difficult for Him to deal with, and to transfigure? He can make it shine with glory.

Do you believe it? My friend, here is surely the final victory of faith — to be able to say, 'The Lord God omnipotent reigneth,' to cry it aloud, not only when life is kind and tender and smiling, and the time of the singing of birds is come and the flowers appear on the earth, but even more when the night is dark, and you are far from home, and the proud waters are going over your soul; to cry it then, not weakly nor diffidently nor uncertainly, but vehemently and passionately and with the ring of faith in every syllable of it — 'The Lord God omnipotent reigneth. Hallelujah!'

This is the Lord God who has come again to the gate of your life and mine today. This is the Lord God who claims the right to reign, and from whose patient, haunting pursuit we can never in this world get free. Behold, He stands at the the door, and knocks. While the sands of time are running out and the hurrying days mould our destiny, He stands at the door and knocks. Tenderer than the kiss of a little child, mightier than the flashing lightnings of Heaven, He stands at the door and knocks. What will our answer be? 'You, out there at the door, you who have been haunting and troubling me all these years — begone, and leave me in peace!' Is that it? Or is it not rather this? 'Blessed and glorious Lord Almighty, dear loving Christ of God — come! Come now. My life is yours. See here is the throne. Oh, Christ, take your power — and reign!'

III

Why Be a Christian?

Who is like unto thee, O people saved by the Lord?'
— DEUT. xxxiii. 29.

IS THERE NOT SOMETHING LIKE THE SOUND OF A TRUMPET IN
that? Here surely is a word of God to stir and thrill our
hearts.

For you see what it does. It takes religion, the life that is
lived for God, it takes (to bring this right over without delay
into the light of the gospel revelation) the life in Christ, and
it lifts it up before the eyes of the world, and cries, 'There —
can you beat that?' It takes a life which God has redeemed
and blessed and regenerated, any such life — it matters not
where it is found, whether in the courts of the house of the
Lord, or in a garret in a slum — it takes that life, and holds
it high, and challenges the world to produce anything like
it. 'Bring out your best,' it dares the world, 'bring out your
very best and highest — and see how that Christ-redeemed
life will dwarf it! For there, in the humblest soul on which
God has set His seal, is something that you simply cannot
achieve, cannot even touch — and never shall.' 'Who is like
unto thee, O people saved by the Lord?'

So declares the Word of God. Do we agree with it?
Certainly it is a daring challenge. It is a vast and sweeping
claim. Do you think it is perhaps too daring, too self-assured?
Let us look into it. Let us cross-question it. Let us come
down to particulars and ask: In what specific ways does the
Christian life beat all the rest? Just how is it superior?
Clearly if we can answer this quesion, the other question —

31

Why be a Christian? — automatically answers itself.

What I propose to do, then, is to suggest four definite points — there are far more, of course, but we shall confine ourselves today to these — at which the Christian life surpasses every other.

First, I am prepared to maintain this, that the Christian life is *happier than any other*.

'Well now,' says someone rather sceptically, 'I find it hard to credit that! Indeed, I may as well be frank and say I don't believe it. To me the Christian life seems cramping and restricting and forbidding. Look at So-and-so! He is a worthy Christian. But did you ever see anything so dull and sombre and insipid? The happiest life in the world? I can't believe it.'

Alas, that such an argument should have some show of reason! But it has. There are Christians who, by the dreariness and joylessness of their religion, its lack of spirit and of radiance, are betraying the Master they are pledged to serve, and giving Christ a bad name amongst men.

That is what some of them did for Francis Thompson. He had seen in his youth a good deal of this lack-lustre religion; and he ran off with the thought that Christianity was a prison-house, and Christ the world's master kill-joy. In his own wild words —

> 'I fled Him, down the nights and down the days;
> I fled Him, down the arches of the years;
> I fled Him, down the labyrinthine ways
> Of my own mind; and in the mist of tears
> I hid from Him, and under running laughter.'

And he makes the reason for his flight from Christ quite explicit:

> 'Yet was I sore adread
> Lest, having Him, I must have naught beside.'

Today there are thousands holding off from Christ for the very same reason. And what one longs to say to them is this: 'Don't be put off by these gloomy caricatures of Christianity. For God's sake don't judge Jesus, the King of joy, by them! Try the real thing — not that miserable parody of the reality — try the real thing, make friends with Jesus, stand where Peter and John and Andrew stood and look into His eyes, listen to the music of His voice, answer His challenge, rise and follow, and you will find it the happiest life on earth!'

Look at it like this. What would you consider to be the three greatest enemies of happiness in this world? I think they are worry, boredom, and self-centredness.

Worry. Think of the multitudes who are hag-ridden by that, always conscious of a sword of Damocles hanging above their heads, overwhelmed and overburdened and with no reserves of inner peace, half-hypnotised by life's anxious cares, and totally unable to get free.

Boredom. Think of the folk for whom life is just a listless, zestless, plodding along, with never a lift of the heart, never a song on the lips, never a thrill in the soul, never a shout of praise to God for the sheer joy of being alive. There is no 'mounting up with wings as eagles' for them: they pass through the world indifferent, apathetic, bored.

And self-centredness. Take the man who is always in the right, always slightly superior, always brooding about others' stupidity, always irritated and nervy because he cannot forget himself nor give his critical faculty a rest. The self-centred man never knows what peace means, let alone the deep calm of joy.

So you have these three great enemies of happiness — worry, boredom, self-centredness. But now — this is the point — Christianity slays them all!

Worry — Christianity finishes that. How? God is on the throne, it says. You are in God the Father's hand, it says.

And even though the worst should happen, even though your whole scheme of things were to collapse, even though the very heavens were to crash in ruin, nothing — I beg you to get that clear, literally and absolutely nothing — can pluck you, or your dear ones, out of the great Father's keeping!

Boredom — Christianity finishes that. How? By filling your life full with the glory of a friendship whose wonders are unending. Do you think the first disciples were ever bored in the company of Jesus? They were ashamed of themselves often, mystified and puzzled and taken out of their depth quite frequently, sometimes furiously excited, occasionally even frightened — but bored? Never. What a thrilling Companion He was! They would have gone through the world with Him if He had asked them. And when, after Pentecost, He did ask them, right through the world they went. He is the same thrilling Companion still. You never know what romance may happen next, when it is the Christ of God who is with you on the road.

Self-centredness — Christianity finishes that. How? By taking you, once and for all, right out of yourself. By sending your critical faculty through the baptism of the Holy Spirit of love. By bursting the petty horizons, and shattering the narrower ways, and thrusting you forth, a crusader with the saints, with Christ going on before!

Think of it: the three greatest enemies of happiness — all slain by Christianity, and buried too deep for any resurrection. And that is the life which Jesus offers. 'Who is like unto thee — for happiness — O people saved by the Lord?'

There, then, is our first answer to the question, Why be a Christian? The Christian life is happier than any other. But I can imagine someone saying, 'Is that an adequate motive? Might it not, indeed, be just a species of selfishness to embrace Christianity for the happiness it gives?' Clearly we must attempt a further answer. I ask you now to consider a second point, of a totally different kind. The Christian life is *harder than any other*.

'What do you say?' asks someone. 'Harder? To be a Christian? But I always thought Christianity was easy, that anyone could be a Christian, almost without turning a hair. You just sign your name, you accept a creed, you go to Church now and again, you say an occasional prayer. Harder?' goes on the critic. 'Will you tell me, then, what precisely your religion is costing *you*? Take the past week, the past month, the past year — in what way has professing Christ made things harder for you?'

That is the challenge. Now once again we have to be quite frank, and admit that there is some cause for it. For there is a type of character which turns to Christ's religion for shelter and comfort — and for nothing else. It is possible, fatally possible, to worship Jesus without obeying Jesus — like the man who will piously attend dozens of religious meetings, and yet be irritable in his own home. It is possible to sing,

> 'Jesus, the very thought of Thee
> With the sweetness fills my breast;
> But sweeter far Thy face to see,
> And in Thy presence rest'

without having once asked ourselves if there are not things in our life and character that that holy Presence, if it once came anywhere near us, would burn to shreds. It is possible to take a great bouquet of flowers, an armful of fine-sounding phrases, and camouflage the cross. I do want to put this as strongly as I can: criticise religion if you will, argue it, debate it, cross-question it — but for God's sake don't sentimentalise it. Don't make the name of Jesus of Nazareth sweet or sickly! Don't taint Christ's strong religion with unreality. One day when Jesus was going down the street, a woman cried after Him, 'Blessed be she who bore Thee, and the breast where Thy head lay!' But Jesus turned round at once, and rebuked the sentimental speech. 'Nay,' He exclaimed, 'say rather, blessed are they who hear the word of God, and do it.'

A decadent religion may be easy; but the real Christian life is definitely harder than any other. Some of our Christian brethren in Europe today have been proving that: for bitter beyond words have been the sacrifices they have had to face through their brave refusal to acknowledge any King or Head of the Church but Jesus Christ.

But we do not need to look so far for examples. Every man who is taking Jesus seriously knows that this is fact. It can sometimes be desperately difficult to do the genuinely Christian thing.

Think, for instance, how Jesus has tightened up the ethical standard.

The world used to say, 'If you do not kill, nor steal, nor break the social code, that is all that is required of you.' Then Jesus came. 'I say, No!' declared Jesus. 'If you have one angry thought, one scornful feeling, one hidden, lurking resentment against your brother' — ah! how His words find us out — 'you are sinning against God!'

The world said, 'If you do not break the seventh commandment, your character will stand.' Jesus came. 'I say, No,' was His ruling. 'If so much as one impure desire finds lodgment and welcome in your heart, even if it is never more than a mere thought, you are sinning against God.'

The world said, 'If you do just what you are paid for in this life, if you go the mile that duty demands, you can feel content.' 'No,' cried Jesus, 'My religion is to mean more than duty; it is to begin on the other side of duty. What about the extra mile? Are you willing for that? If not, you are sinning against God.'

And so, at every point, you can see Jesus heightening the

moral ideal. Take Him seriously, and you are in for the hardest life in the world.

'Well surely,' cries someone in astonishment, 'that is a queer reason for recommending Christianity! A strange answer to the question, Why be a Christian? You have given your case away. It is a first-rate reason for *not* being a Christian!'

I wonder. Sometimes the very difficulty of a task is its most magnetic appeal. Is there any young man here who is wanting the secret of an easy passage through this world? Then you may as well shut your New Testament now, and never open it again: for you will not find it there. But thank God, you are not really wanting that. You are a far bigger man. You are wanting adventure. You are out for a life that will keep you on the stretch. You are wanting a Leader who will put you on your mettle every day you live. I offer you Jesus. Son of man, stand upon thy feet, and Christ will speak with thee! And for this — for the glory of the hardness of it — 'who is like unto thee, O people saved by the Lord?'

So it is happier than any other — the Christian life — and it is harder than any other. Will you take now a third factor into consideration? The life in Christ is *holier than any other*.

This is a word, it must be admitted, for which many people today have but little liking. Ask the average young man if he would care to be known as a 'holy' person, and probably his reaction will be one of two things. Either he will laugh at you, or else he will be horrified at you. 'Holy? No, thank you. Anything you like but that!'

But wait a moment. The word in popular parlance may have lost caste; but it is worth while, as Dr. Fosdick has recently reminded us, going behind it to its original meaning. What was that? Wholesome, healthy. Holiness means inward health. It means healthy instincts, healthy emotions, every part of life in a disciplined, balanced, wholesome condition. It means, in short, to put it psychologically, an integrated personality.

Is that not the greatest need of thousands today — something to pull life together and integrate it, to deal drastically with the inward conflicts that damage spiritual health so seriously; something to eliminate the discords and repressions and dangerous complexes, and to bring everything into the harmony and unity of strong, clean, vigorous health, emotional and moral; something (to use the word in its true meaning) to make them holy?

And why was Jesus ever called the Great Physician, if not because He alone can produce this kind of vital health? He does that in two ways. He gives life a new purpose. And He fills life with a new power.

A purpose: that is, a sense of direction, the grip of a great ideal which gathers up all the soul's scattered, turbulent energies, focusing them on one thing — 'Seek ye first the Kingdom of God!'

And the power: a vitalising, supernatural strength flooding a man's being, and sending him out like a conqueror to smash his most stubborn besetting sin, with the light of God in his eyes, and the cry upon his lips — 'I can do all things through Him who strengthens me!'

With that purpose and that power, Christ integrates a man. No longer need he pass his days lamenting the burden and the chaos of a sadly divided personality, like the poor pathetic creature in the Gospel, whose name was Legion — 'for we are many.' In Christ, he is a whole man now. Emotional health, moral health, spiritual health, they are all his. He is 'holy.' And for this — 'who is like unto thee, O people saved by the Lord?'

It is happier than any other — this life, harder than any other, holier than any other. One last claim let me make. The Christian life is *more hopeful than any other*.

More hopeful — why? Because while every other life is bounded by this little world, Christianity has all the windows open towards immortality. Naturalism, speaking in the voice of Bertrand Russell, can only say that 'no fire, no heroism, no intensity of thought and feeling can preserve an individual life beyond the grave; that all the labours of the ages, all the devotion, all the inspiration, all the noonday brightness of human genius, are destined to extinction in the vast death of the solar system, and that the whole temple of man's achievement must inevitably be buried beneath the debris of a universe in ruins.' But Christianity sweeps that horror of darkness from its soul, and stands facing out towards eternity. And when the day comes which Shakespeare's Prospero foretold, when

> The cloud-capp'd towers, the gorgeous palaces,
> The solemn temples, the great globe itself,
> Yea, all which it inherit, shall dissolve
> And, like this insubstantial pageant faded,
> Leave not a rack behind' —

then, declares Christ, then more than ever, the soul of man will go marching, marching, marching on to God!

There are some today who would take this item out of the Christian creed, and leave us the rest: some who would banish from our hearts every gleam of glory from the world beyond. They know not what they are doing! Take the eternal hope away, and you have no evangel left. 'If in this life only we have hope in Christ, we are of all men most miserable.'

No immortality? Then dust and ashes are the goal we are making for. No life everlasting? Then when you said goodbye to your dear one entering the river, it was final, an utterly irrevocable farewell: never will reunion happen, nowhere the beloved come to your arms again.

'If I had believed that,' said a man to me one day when he had lost his dearest upon earth, 'if I had believed that, I think I should have gone mad. But oh, thank God for Christ!' Life and immortality to light!

I beg you — every time you think of death and parting and the losing of the angel faces, get down on your knees and thank God for Christ! For He has shown you death defeated, and parting ended, and the angel faces happy and smiling in God's Heaven.

> 'O blessed hope! with this elate,
>   Let not our hearts be desolate,
>   But, strong in faith, in patience wait
>   Until He come.'

'Who is like unto thee, O people saved by the Lord?' It is a happier life than any other, a harder life, a holier life, an infinitely more hopeful life. Why be a Christian? Is anyone hesitating? Does some one need just one word more to carry him into the Kingdom? Then let that word be this. It is not only a happy, a hard, a holy, a hopeful life. It is *His* life!

That is what you are being offered — the very life which Jesus lived, the very eternity where Jesus reigns forever. His life! And He is offering it to you Himself. To you by name He offers it. Listen, when you say your prayers tonight. Listen, when you are alone, and the service of this hour is but a memory. Listen, when your soul is quiet. And it may be that, ringing clear through the dark, there will come a Voice and you will hear Him speak your name. And then — 'Brother, sister,' He will say, 'I give you this — My life, My Spirit, My love and joy and peace, I give them all to you.' What a day tomorrow would be if that happened between your soul and Christ tonight! And how radiant all life's tomorrows, until the last great daybreak come!

IV

Sacrifice and Song

'And when the burnt-offering began, the song of the Lord began also with the trumpets.' — 2 CHRON. xxix. 27.

THERE MUST BE FEW PEOPLE IN THIS WORLD WHO CAN SAY that life for them has turned out exactly as they planned. There must be very few, perhaps none, who have seen everything working out according to the time-table and schedule of their dreams.

It is one of the commonest experiences of life, that men set their hearts upon the achievement of some strong desire or hope, and then providence says 'No', or at least gives something totally different.

Here is a youth who wanted to be a doctor; but his father died, and he had to leave school and go out and earn a wage to help to keep the home going — and there will be no university now for him. Here is a business man who hoped to make his business a triumphant success; but the competition was fiercer than he had bargained for, and he began to find himself being left behind in the race; and the years are passing, and the burden and heat of the day are telling upon him, and he has lost some of the old resilience and buoyancy, and knows that he will never make much of that business now. Here is a man who wanted love and a home and children; and he has been given a road that will be solitary to the very end. Here is a woman who wanted to be a nurse in India, and she has got an office-desk in the town in which she was born. Here is someone made for art and

41

music and all lovely things, yet tied to a life of drudgery, twelve hours in the day and seven days in the week.

It is a queer, incalculable thing, this life; and for few, for very few, does it work out in detail just as they had planned. Sooner or later, one fact confronts every pilgrim on the road, the fact of the discipline of hopes denied and plans defeated. Something in us, something in our hearts and hopes, has to be the burnt offering on the altar: life demands it, providence decrees it. And what happens then? Is it not often this, that when the burnt offering begins, the song finishes, and all life's music is gone?

But look — it was so different here in Israel! 'When the burnt offering began, the song of the Lord began also with the trumpets.'

This was a memorable hour in the nation's history. Read what precedes this in the story, and you will see that for half a generation, right through the reign of King Ahaz, there had been a disastrous slump in morals and religion. But now Ahaz was dead; and a man after God's own heart, Hezekiah, was on the throne. He purged the land of its abuses; then summoned his people to a solemn service of rededication in the Temple. And the climax of that service was the moment which this text describes.

Can you picture it? Yonder stands the high altar, with the sacrifice laid upon it waiting for the fire. A vast concourse crowds the temple courts: they stand there, hushed and eager and expectant — for they know what that burnt offering on the altar represents. It represents themselves. It signifies their own life-dedication, as they offer themselves, body and soul, a willing sacrifice, to the God whom for years they have forsaken. Now before the waiting throng, a solitary figure moves forward to the altar, carrying the lighted brand; the fire leaps up, and the offering on the altar goes up in flame. And suddenly in that dramatic moment, the tense silence is shattered, and from the packed throng rises a great burst of jubilant music, peal after peal of triumphant melody. 'When the burnt offering began, the song of the Lord began also, with the trumpets.'

Today I want to say that, if you and I belong to God, this story can happen all over again, at altars more personal and private and individual. That the sternly disciplining touch of pain and disappointment is an almost inescapable element in life we have already seen: life will not always run our way. But here is the great discovery — that these sore and difficult things, instead of impoverishing, can positively enrich; that the hard self-denials we have to make, and the frustrations which our hopes endure, can actually, under God, put into our life something of tremendous value which was not there before, a deeper tone, a finer touch, a nobler music; and that, when in our experience the burnt offering begins, then for us — perhaps not until then — the song of the Lord may begin also with the trumpets.

Do you remember the old familiar legend of the German baron who built his castle by the Rhine? From crag to crag and from turret to turret he hung wires, hoping that the winds, as they blew upon this great Aeolian harp, might make sweet music. Long and patiently he waited, and round his castle winds from the four corners of heaven blew: and still no music came. But one night there arose a hurricane, tossing the Rhine to fury; the black sky was stabbed with lightning and the thunder rolled, the earth trembled, and the winds were mad and shrieking. The baron went to his great castle door to view the terrifying scene — when hark! the sound of music, like angels singing through the storm. And suddenly he realised what had happened. His harp, strung from crag to crag, had come to life at last. The tempest had given it a soul. That oft-told tale goes down to the heart of life's deep mystery. How often it is only when trouble comes that a man's true quality stands revealed!

When the burnt offering — the sore, costly thing — begins, the song of the Lord begins also.

Here, let us say, is a man who in his youth dreamed a dream: he set his heart on attaining success and distinction in his profession. But success and distinction, as the world counts them, have never come to him, no plaudits of the crowd, no glare of flattery or fame. Has he then failed? If he is no longer searching for the world's applause, if he has grown content to work on quite obscure, if he has seen issues that lie deeper far than human praise or blame, if he has learnt to live by the faith that life's true values are spiritual — character, and kindness, and cheerfulness, and humility, and compassion — has he really failed? Failed! The man is a most triumphant success. And round the altar of the burnt-offering, that daily immolation of himself, there is the music of the trumpets.

Or here is a girl who was once, to all intents and purposes, utterly frivolous, living for pleasure and for self and nothing else; and then she got married, and God gave her a child; and one day her child fell ill, and there was a great hush in the home, and for days and nights the angel of death was hovering there, and the dark valley of the shadow seemed closing round her little one. Then, marvellously, the shadow receded, and the knock of death's angel at the door of the home was heard no longer, and healing came, and restoration; and from that hour, people have noticed something in that woman's life which was never there before — a new poise and dignity, a deeper tone, a tenderer and more radiant serenity. What has happened? Simply this — that when the burnt offering began, the song of the Lord has begun also.

I am not suggesting, mark you, that this always or inevitably happens. It is quite obvious that it does not. Sometimes trouble and disappointment and heartache produce a purely negative reaction. Sometimes the burnt offering leads only to bitterness and self-pity and resentment. It all depends on whether your life, at some point, can be laid open towards God.

One of the bravest, most poignant letters ever written tells of the death of Dr. Edward Wilson, Scott's companion in the Antarctic. Scott himself, dying in his tent, was the writer. 'If this letter reaches you, Bill and I will have gone out together. We are very near it now, and I should like you to know how splendid he was at the end — everlastingly cheerful and ready to sacrifice himself for others, never a word of blame to me for leading him into this mess. His eyes have a comfortable blue look of hope and his mind is peaceful with the satisfaction of his faith in regarding himself as a part of the great scheme of the Almighty. I can do no more to comfort you than to tell you that he died as he lived, a brave true man — the best of comrades, and staunchest of friends.' Will you think of that — for does not the secret of spiritual victory in the day of sacrifice lie there — 'his eyes with a comfortable blue look of hope, and his mind peaceful with his faith that he is part of the great scheme of the Almighty'? It is on that kind of faith — for each and all of us — that everything in the last resort depends, the faith that our own life, with all its difficulties and problems and hard self-denials and defeated hopes, has nevertheless a place in God's great plan, and that even in the most hurting experiences love almighty is in control. Without that faith, life is bound to lead to bitterness. But with it, the sacrifice becomes the signal for the song.

And so I repeat, it all depends on whether our life is open to God, whether we are ready under all circumstances to say, 'O God, not my will, but Thine be done!' Can you look up from your knees, when you are at your prayers, into the face of God the Father, and say — 'Lord, ask anything Thou choosest, anything at all, and if it is Thy will for me, I will accept it! Even if it means some terribly difficult denial of my own plans and dreams, even if it drives me down a lonelier, harder road than I ever thought I should have to travel — if it is Thy will, O God, for me, with unwavering heart I will accept it' — can you say that, and mean it?

You see, we have gone deeper now. The burnt-offering we are thinking of now is something more than the inevitable discipline life puts us through. It is the surrender of our will to a higher will. It is the crushing down of our personal inclinations that our duty to God may be supreme. It is the dedication of every dream and desire to the mastery of Christ. It is the consecration of life to the religion of the cross. And that is the costliest burnt offering of all.

And that is why on many altars, and perhaps upon our own, it has never yet been offered. 'I refuse to make such a surrender of myself,' we say. 'I will not have my inclinations thus overridden. I will not hand over the planning and controlling of my life to a higher authority. I will not bring myself to say:

'The dearest idol I have known,
      Whate'er that idol be,
   Help me to tear it from Thy throne.'

I will not do it! For if I did, what would be left to me? It would spoil everything. The zest of life, the liberty, the keen edge of its most thrilling pleasures, would all be gone. That burnt offering would stifle all the music!'

If only something or someone could convince us that that is the profoundest of mistakes! Cling to those inclinations, refuse to have God interfering, plan out your heart's desire — does happiness lie that way? Surely life has taught us enough to make us see that that way only restlessness lies, and a dreadful unsatisfied feeling, and a hunger for something more than the poor prizes of this earth.

And if you are wanting happiness — and it is only natural

that you should — if it is peace you are hungry for, and the ending of the strained, restless feeling which is like a fever in the soul and a shadow on the face, if you would like a heart not driven this way and that, but steady and satisfied and serene, will you remember what Dante said, the deepest, truest thing of all — 'In His will is our peace'? I beg you to be sure of this, that however hard and difficult and sacrificial the road of that will may seem, it is down that thorny and unlikely road that there is waiting the great discovery, the very thing which has been sought everywhere else in vain — the peace of being able to forget oneself, the happiness of a heart content, and the serenity of God which passeth understanding. Our true life, our Christian effectiveness, our share in the joy which is the Spirit's most characteristic fruit, will always depend on the degree in which we surrender, or fail to surrender, our inclinations to the final control of God. Spiritual power will always vary in direct proportion to spiritual dedication. 'In His will is our peace'; and in our burnt offering of ourselves on the altar of that will is the song of the Lord, with the trumpets.

I cannot ask anyone to believe this, or to accept the truth of it, just by hearing it: it is far too different from our ordinary way of viewing things for that. But I can ask someone here to put his own life, her own life, into it, and to make the experiment at least. None who ever did that failed to find it true.

Think of St. Francis, who dedicated himself to the crucified Christ with such a passion of devotion that they said the very wounds of Jesus appeared upon his flesh; it was out of the throes of that experience that he composed his great Canticle of the Sun, one of the most glorious outbursts of praise that ever broke from human lips:

> 'All creatures of our God and King,
>   Lift up your voice and with us sing
>   Alleluia!'

The stigmata in his hands, and the Hallelujah in his heart!
The burnt-offering — and the song! Think of Paul and Silas,
and of their first experience of Europe — the Philippian
dungeon, the lash, the rack, the torture, and then — 'at
midnight Paul and Silas prayed, and sang praises unto God'.
The burnt offering and the song! Think of Mary of Nazareth,
called from her girlhood dreams to travel the road of a
lonely destiny, to be the mother of Jesus; think of how she
shrank back trembling from the call and from the sword
that was to pierce her heart, until at last she bowed her
head, and said, 'Behold, the handmaid of the Lord; be it
unto me according to Thy word.' And then, immediately
thereafter, the Magnificat! 'My soul doth magnify the Lord,
and my spirit hath rejoiced in God my Saviour.' The burnt-
offering and the song! Best of all, think of Jesus. 'Father,
let this cup pass! Let this cup pass!' And His sweat was like
blood. But then — the quiet acceptance. 'If this cup may
not pass away from Me, except I drink it, Thy will be done.'
And then, with lifted head, on like a conqueror to the cross
and the victory — and all the herald angels singing to welcome Him home! The burnt offering and the song!

You cannot accept this until you have tried it; but none
whoever tested it failed to find it true.

For God stands loyally to His word; and the one thing
that can never happen is this — that you should make the
sacrifice, and take the difficult road of consecration, and
then find that God had let you down, and that there was no
spiritual power, no inward happiness, no peace of heart as
your reward. That, on the guarantee of Christ, will never
happen.

And mark you, it is no broken melody, nor any plaintive
minor cadence, that is the music born of self-sacrifice: it is
'the song of the Lord — *with the trumpets.*' It is not only,
said Paul, being a conqueror over yourself: it is being more
than conqueror. It is not taking up your daily cross with

stoic resignation: it is finding, as Samuel Rutherford found, that the cross is 'such a burden as wings are to a bird, or sails to a boat'. The joy that comes on the difficult road is real joy. The happiness that lies in putting God's will first is genuine happiness. It is no pale, wan, pious pretence, no forced cheerfulness, no making the best of a bad job. It is really being happy. It has red blood in it. It is positive, and eager, and magnificently alive. It is the song of the Lord — with the trumpets!

And the reason is, that in Christianity at least, you are not sacrificing for anything so cold or abstract as duty or dogma or the dictates of a code: you are doing it for the best Friend you ever had. You are doing it for God's splendid Christ, the dear divine Lover of your soul. Oh, we need to get the note of adoration back into our religion! We need to recapture the thrill of the friendship of Jesus. We need to stand on the shore at break of day, and see Him coming back to us after the dark night of all our base denials, to hear the voice that says, 'Lovest thou Me?' Once we have been there with Jesus, we shall not want to talk of sacrifices any longer; but we shall say — with David Livingstone and James Chalmers and many another — that any price we have to pay to make God's will our own is not really sacrifice at all, for we would rather be with Christ than anywhere else in the world. And then indeed the burnt offering will go up to God with the song of the Lord and the trumpets.

There is a very beautiful poem, which seems to me to sum up and express everything I have tried to say today. It is the story of a soul that shrank from the difficult road, but finally accepted it, and found there a happiness unspeakable.

'I said, "Let me walk in the fields."
    He said, "Nay, walk in the town."
I said, "There are no flowers there."
    He said, "No flowers, but a crown."

I said, "But the sky is black,
    There is nothing but noise and din."
But He wept as He sent me back,
    "There is more," He said, "there is sin."

I said, "But the air is thick,
    And fogs are veiling the sun."
He answered, "Yet hearts are sick,
    And souls in the dark undone."

I said, "I shall miss the light,
    And friends will want me, they say."
He answered me, "Choose tonight,
    If I am to miss you, or they."

I cast one look at the fields,
    Then set my face to the town.
He said, "My child, do you yield?
    Will you leave the flowers for the crown?"

Then into His hand went mine,
    And into my heart came He,
And I walk in a light divine
    The path that I feared to see.'

So it always is. And so it may be for someone here this
morning. When the burnt offering begins, the song of the
Lord will begin also, with the trumpets.

V

The Universality of Jesus

'And a superscription also was written over Him in
letters of Greek, and Latin, and Hebrew, THIS IS THE
KING OF THE JEWS.' — LUKE xxiii. 38.

IT WAS THE COMMON CUSTOM IN THOSE DAYS, WHEN A CRIMINAL
was executed, publicly to placard his crime. A brief description of the charge on which the man had been condemned
was written out and nailed to the gallows itself, in order
that passers-by, looking up and seeing him there, might know
what had brought him to that end. As the Man on the centre
cross on Calvary had been condemned for claiming kingly
rights for Himself, a claim which obviously neither Caesar
nor Judaism could tolerate, the words of the charge stood
written above His head — 'This is Jesus the King.'

But why the three languages? No doubt they were used,
in the first instance, to make sure that everyone in the crowd
— for Jerusalem in that Passover time was packed with
visitors from all parts of the world — should be able to read
and understand. But another hand than Pilate's had been
working there. Providence had a hand in it. For Greek,
Latin, and Hebrew were the three great languages of the
world. Each of them represented a whole panorama of
history. Each was the vehicle and expression of a great
world-movement. Each stood for a different, dominant idea,
each was the servant of that idea. Each was a tide which
carried the spirits of men. And each was at the cross to
proclaim it: 'This is Jesus the King.' Do you see what
Providence was intending? Everything that the Greek idea in

history stood for — Jesus was King there. Everything that the Roman idea in history stood for — Jesus was King there. Everything that the Hebrew idea in history stood for — Jesus was King there. Verily, on His head are many crowns!

It was written in Greek. Now Greek was the language of Culture. Down the centuries the history of the Greeks had stood for culture. Francis Thompson once said, 'Prose is clay; poetry the white, molten metal.' It was the Greeks who put the white, molten metal into life, the poetry of things, the culture. From that little land, set in its Mediterranean seas, there burst through the clay of life a beauty which was dazzling and indescribable, and along with beauty there came intellect, keen-edged, powerful, godlike. In art, they flamed out in Pheidias, creator of the great sculptures whose perfection is still, after centuries of imitation, absolutely unrivalled, the marvel and the despair of the world. In thought and intellect, they towered up in Plato, Socrates, and Aristotle, who have set the pace for all other thinkers for ever. In poetry,

'The isles of Greece, the isles of Greece!
Where burning Sappho loved and sung,'

those isles, that happy mainland, have been the fount and spring of a music, a rhythm, a loveliness, which will go singing their way down the centuries as long as there is a sense of beauty in the souls of men. The Greeks were the genius people, who created the culture of the world. When Alexander the Great set out on his campaigns, he told Aristotle that it was his ambition to make all men everywhere Greeks. He failed in that; but he did succeed in sowing the seeds of Greek culture everywhere. We today, two thousand years on, are immeasurably their debtors. The whole world is in their debt. And the language which had to carry all that weight of glory, the language in which all that beauty and intellect and genius were concentrated, was the language that these men in their sea-girt home had hammered out for themselves. Greek was the language of culture.

And it was written on the cross in Greek — 'This is Jesus the King.' In other words, Jesus was claiming the realm of culture for His own. Jesus is King there.

But is He? There is a type of culture in the world today which definitely leaves Jesus out. There is a culture which is frankly irreligious. It disowns the divinity of Jesus, and dethrones the ethics of Jesus. It acknowledges no God save the spirit of man himself. This is the culture which numbered amongst its protagonists Swinburne, whose glorious verse descends sometimes into a mere scream of petulant irritation at Jesus. 'Glory to man in the highest!' he cried, in terrible parody of the angels' song. This is the culture which W. K. Clifford, Huxley's contemporary and friend, was championing when he exclaimed — 'From the innermost depth of every soul, the face of our father man looks out upon us, and says, "Before Jehovah was, I am".' At the great Jerusalem Missionary Conference it was stressed again and again that the really dangerous foe which Christianity is facing today is not Buddhism, nor Islam, nor the worship of any other god, but this world-wide anti-religious culture which owns no God at all.

It spreads itself over every department of life — art, philosophy, politics, industry, literature. Thousands of people are feeling today that a great mass of modern literature, for all its undoubted skill and artistry, is strangely unsatisfying. What is the reason? Surely the reason is that so much of it is written without any sort of background of God. Now the background of life *is* God; and therefore books which claim to be 'realistic', and yet have no inkling of that background, are not realistic at all. It is an extraordinary thing that a novelist should be able to write five or six hundred pages, tracing in all its ins and outs and most intimate details the life-story of his hero or heroine, without a single word to suggest that either the author or the character he is portraying has so much as heard of God or the religious sense.

Sometimes indeed this type of culture does express its views on religion, generally in a rather patronising way. But Jesus Christ wants no one's patronage. He wants no admiring testimonial. He wants the surrender of a man's soul! 'Oh, Doctor,' said an effusive young lady once to Jowett of Balliol, 'do tell me — what do you think about God?' to which the Master replied — 'That, my dear young lady, is a very unimportant question; the only thing that signifies is what God thinks about me.' Christ courts no man. Christ commands him.

John Owen, the Puritan, was perfectly right when he said — anticipating here the message of that great modern prophet, Karl Barth — that the main barrier between the human soul and Christ is simply pride, the self-sufficient, superior feeling which will not go down on its knees and cry, 'God be merciful to me a sinner.' There is many a man today who, rather than stand thus in Christ's debt, refuses the outstretched hand of saving grace and leaves Christ out altogether.

One of the most dangerous features of this irreligion culture is its tendency to elevate cleverness above goodness If only a man in his own walk of life has a touch of genius that, it holds, more than atones for any defects in his ethical standards. But this quite certainly is not the view of Jesus. Nor is it the view of any Christian who is taking Jesus seriously. It is surely a strange and discreditable idea that because a man happens to write better, or paint better, or compose better poetry than his neighbour, he is automatically exempted from certain of the moral standards to which he neighbour is expected to conform. That is not only absurd: it is a dangerous heresy. For in the realm of culture, Jesus claims, and rightly claims, to be King.

It comes to this. Everywhere, in art, literature, ethics, society, our standard is to be the character of Christ. When we start bringing all our culture to that test — the test of Jesus' white, scorching purity with which nothing unclean can live, the test of Jesus' absolute honesty before which everything that is merely sensational and nastily suggestive is made to look unutterably mean, the test of Jesus' cross where in a passion of self-sacrifice He condemned all self-seeking for ever — then we shall have our faces towards the truth. Then in the realm of culture, Christ will have the place that is His due. They wrote it on the cross in Greek — 'This is Jesus the King.'

It was written in Latin. Now Latin was the language of Government. Down the centuries the history of the Romans had stood for law and government. From their splendid city, set on its seven hills, they looked north, south, east, and west, and ruled the whole known earth. They sent their engineers out to build the great roads, the trade and commerce routes to the farthest corners of their dominions. They sent their marching legions out, to subjugate all the nations and bring them under one command. They sent their colonists out, to plant the Roman flag on every shore. They sent their civil servants out, to maintain law and order throughout the world. And so they built up the greatest empire the world has ever seen. They had such a genius for law and government that every system of law today, after the lapse of centuries, looks back to the Roman system as its parent. And the language which had to carry all that majesty of law, the language in which the world was taught to think imperially, was the language which these sturdy descendants of Romulus first framed. Latin was the language of government.

And it was written on the the cross in Latin — 'This is Jesus the King.' In other words, Jesus was claiming the realm of government for His own. Jesus is King there — King of nations.

But is He? There is a type of rule which ignores Jesus. There is a spirit in national and international affairs which would hold Jesus at arm's length. When the idea of the League of Nations was first germinating in men's minds a suggestion was made that the Covenant of the League should contain some reference to Almighty God. That suggestion was turned down as quite impossible. And today the attitude in many quarters is, 'Don't bring religion into politics', — which, when you reduce it to its practical effect, means this, 'Don't take Christ too seriously!'

When will it be realised that this exclusion of Jesus from the sphere of secular government, this rigid separation between things secular and things sacred, this department-alising of life which warns Christ, 'Thus far and no farther,' is always fatal? It is fatal because at the heart of it there is a radical insincerity, the insincerity which runs life on two gears, and is continually changing over from one to the other; the blindness which will not see that there are not and cannot be two kinds of truth, but that Jesus must either be King everywhere, in every sacred and every secular sphere, or else King nowhere at all; that, in short, your only alternatives are either to apply the gospel to every single one of life's relationships or else scrap the gospel altogether, and that there is no third option.

Jesus, in this realm of government, has a right to be King. Everyone remembers Napoleon's words: 'Alexander, Caesar, Charlemagne, and myself founded empires. But on what did we rest the creations of our genius? Upon force. Jesus Christ founded His empire upon love; and, at this hour, millions of men would die for Him.' That is true. For in sheer royalty of soul the Son of Mary stands alone for ever, solitary and unique, born to be King of the universe. There was a day when a Roman centurion went to Jesus, begging Him to come and heal his servant; and do you remember on what he based his claim? 'I perceive,' he said in effect, 'that you, Jesus, just like myself, are a man in authority, with soldiers under you!' In other words, he was quite sure Jesus could do it, because he felt, looking at Jesus, that behind Him there was the majesty of empire, and that here was One born to rule and to command. If only the world had grace enough and vision enough to grasp that fact today! Isaiah, in a dark and lawless age, was given a sudden glimpse from afar of the daybreak of Israel's hope. 'Unto us,' he began to chant, 'a Child is born, unto us a Son is given, *and the government shall be upon His shoulder*.' So God has willed it; and until the world has something better than lip-service for the sovereign rights of Jesus, until 'Crown Him Lord of all' has become more than the fervent sentiment of a hymn and has been accepted as the resolute, daily reaffirmed working creed of every Christian life, until we realise that the only shoulders strong enough to bear the task of governing the destinies of mankind are the shoulders of the Son of God, there will be no peace and no security. He must reign!

Will it ever happen? Is it just an empty dream? One Palm Sunday in the city of Florence four hundred and fifty years ago, Savonarola was preaching to a great multitude. Suddenly in the middle of his discourse he cried aloud, 'It is the Lord's will to give a new Head to this city of Florence!' For a moment he paused, keeping the people in suspense, and then went on: 'The new Head is Christ! Christ seeks to become your King.' And at that the whole multitude, men, women, and children, were on their feet, shouting, 'Long Live Jesus, King of Florence! Long live Jesus the King.' It is there that our hope lies today. Let us give Christ, in the realm of government, the place that is His due. They wrote it on the cross in Latin — 'This is Jesus the King.'

It was written in Hebrew. Now Hebrew was the language of Religion. Down the centuries the history of the Hebrews had stood for revealed religion. Across the dark ages of ancient paganism these people had blazed their trail, carrying wherever they went through that troubled world of many deities the challenge of the one and only God. On the far shores of the Euphrates that challenge was first heard, when a man rose up and left the sweltering squalor of Chaldean heathenism behind, not knowing whither he was going, but sure of the one and only God. In the thundering artillery of Sinai it broke out afresh, bidding men be done with their idols and worship the one and only God. Out of the terrible deserts at a later day came the great prophets, crying, 'Thus saith the Lord', and leading their people back from their wayward wanderings to the one and only God. Still later, in the bitterness of exile, when Zion's glory was past, and Jerusalem just a mass of blackened ruins, one spark still smouldered among the ashes: 'Watchman, what of the night?' they cried, and ever kept peering through the gloom for the coming of the one and only God. The Jews had such a genius for religion that all the world stands in their debt forever. And the language which had to carry all that weight of revelation, the language to which were first committed the oracles of God, was the language which the Jews in their restless, erratic, romantic course down the centuries had fashioned. Hebrew was the language of religion.

And it was written on the cross in Hebrew — 'This is Jesus the King.' In other words, Jesus was claiming the realm of religion for His own. Jesus is King there — King in the sphere of the spirit, revelation's topmost height, God's last word to humanity. 'Neither,' said Peter in his great Jerusalem sermon, 'is there salvation in any other .'

'None other Lamb, none other Name,
 None other Hope in heaven or earth or sea,

None other Hiding-place from guilt and shame,
    None beside Thee.'

Is this the place Christ holds in our personal religion? 'Christ is the greatest character in history,' said that fine essayist, Clutton-Brock, 'just as Hamlet is the greatest character in art.' True; but have you and I nothing better to say about Christ than that? Jesus, said Goethe, is 'the saint, the type and model of all men'. True again; but are we content to leave it there? 'He stood,' said Ernest Renan, 'in the first rank of the grand family of the true sons of God.' Have the souls whom Christ has bought with blood no surer word than that? Yes, they have!

'Jesus, my Lord, my God, my All
    Hear me, blest Saviour, when I call.'

Listen to the seer of Patmos, on the day when he saw heaven opened, and the Word of God riding forth to the conquest of the earth. 'King of kings,' he cried, 'and Lord of lords!' 'Thou canst not comprehend it,' exclaimed Julian the Apostate in Ibsen's *Emperor and Galilean*, 'thou who hast never been under the power of the God-Man. It is more than teaching that He spreads over earth: it is witch-craft that takes the mind captive. They who have been under Him, I believe, can never get free.' No, indeed! They are bound by unbreakable chains for ever; for this is the King in His beauty.

I beg you, in this realm of religion, which means in the deepest intimacies of your life and the most secret fastnesses of your soul — make Jesus King! For please God, a day is coming when the same words which they wrote upon the cross of Calvary are going to be sung around the throne, not now in Greek or Latin or Hebrew, but sung by a great multitude of all nations and kindred and people and tongues, in the perfected language of heaven — 'This is Jesus the King! Lift up your heads, O ye gates; and be ye lift up, ye everlasting doors; and the King of glory shall come in. Hail to the King!' Will our voices be mingling there, on that great crowning day?

VI

Hearsay or Experience?

'Sayest thou this thing of thyself, or did others tell it thee of Me?' — JOHN xviii. 34.

ALL THAT WEEK RUMOUR HAD BEEN BUSY IN THE CAPITAL. Every night excited crowds had been parading the streets, and one word was on every lip — 'The king of the Jews!' No one quite knew where or how the rumour had originated. Some talk there was of a procession of pilgrims from Galilee the Sabbath before, who had come into the city shouting 'Hosanna'. Some said it was they who had started it, but no one seemed to be sure. However it had originated, the rumour was there, flying all round the city. They talked about it in the markets over their bargaining. 'Any further news? Where can He be hiding? Has anyone seen Him?' The Church courts that were in session debated it, and appointed a committee to look into it. The Roman garrison got wind of it, and doubled the guards, and patrolled the streets at night. Everywhere the rumour was flying — 'The King!'

And then it all turned out to be a hoax! 'The coming King? Why, have you not heard? Don't you know who He is? It is the wandering preacher from Nazareth who made a scene in the Temple the other day — the poor deluded soul with His hallucinations and His megalomania — a carpenter's apprentice for a King!' And with that the hopes that had been dashed turned to anger. 'He will suffer for this! Arrested already, is He? Good! He will die for it.' And down the streets to Pilate's palace they poured, to see what was going to happen.

Inside, Pilate and Jesus were face to face. Pilate, too, had heard the rumours about the king. Pilate's sleep had been uneasy for a week because of the rumours about the king. And now there was the Man in front of him; and Pilate, looking at Him, questioning Him, almost began to feel there was something in the rumour after all, half believed it was really true. And yet — how could it be? Oh, if only he could be sure! 'Who are you?' he burst out at last. 'Speak, man! Tell me! *Are* you a king?' Then quietly but searchingly it came, the question of Jesus that goes right to the roots of all religion, 'Pilate, sayest thou this thing of thyself, or did others tell it thee of Me?'

But let us leave Pilate now, for this is Christ's question to everyone of us today, and we must face it. Take that hymn we have just been singing, 'Jesu, Lover of my soul'. I think Jesus would want to know about that. 'Lover of my soul' — 'Sayest thou *this* of thyself, or did Charles Wesley tell it thee of Me?' Are the words about Christ in our hymns and prayers and creeds our own words, beaten out in the fires of our own experience, coming out eager and passionate and really meant, with the zest of a personal discovery behind them; or are we just dully repeating what has been told us by other folk? What, in our religious life, are we founding on — mere hearsay, rumour blown down the centuries from apostolic days, other men's thoughts of Jesus caught and put in cold storage and preserved and handed out to us — is that it? Or are we founding not on that, but on this — a Christ we have spoken to and can speak to daily, face to face and heart to heart; an experience of Jesus thrilling and throbbing and glorious because we can say of it, 'This is my own, my very own'; something that has come to us not on the authority of any Church or creed, not on the authority of our forefathers, not even on the authority of all the millions of believers who have ever lived, but on the authority of God and our souls? 'Sayest thou this thing of thyself, or did others tell it thee of Me?' Is it first-hand experience or second-hand tradition?

I have seen the light that comes into human eyes with the birth of a real experience. I have seen — and how moving it is, only those who have watched it know — a soul growing simply radiant, full of a new tenderness and peace and attractiveness, through a discovery of the friendship of Jesus. I have heard the grateful confession that everything has been different — home life, Church life, personal relationships, everything — since that day when He drew near. And I thank God that, because the wind of the Spirit bloweth where it listeth, this transforming experience is within reach of all.

But there are some who are quite content with a second-hand religion. And that for two reasons.

For one thing, it is *safer*. You always know where you are with it. It will never sin against good form by breaking out with sudden enthusiasms. But the visionary people who claim to have talked with God and seen Christ with their own eyes — it is they who have always been the real disturbers of this earth. 'Why can't they let us alone?' the world asks. Edward Gibbon in his youth had for his tutor that great English mystic, William Law. 'Had not Law's vigorous mind,' wrote Gibbon years afterwards, 'been clouded by enthusiasm, he might be ranked with the most agreeable writers of his time.' There speaks the man who had never seen Christ about the man who had. Chesterton pictures the Church 'rushing through the ages as the winged thunderbolt of an everlasting enthusiasm, a thing without rival or resemblance, and still as new as it is old.' Ah, but that is not what we want, say some: give us something quieter than that, less dangerous and disturbing and incalculable. So they settle down with their second-hand religion, quite content: It is safer.

But another reason attracts them too. It is not only safer,

it is also *easier*. 'I used to be concerned about religion,' said a foreign professor to Henry Drummond, 'but religion is a great subject, and I was busy, and there was little time to settle it for myself: so I became a Catholic, and instead of dabbling any longer in religion myself, just left it to the Church to do everything for me. Once a year I go to Mass.' Yes, it is more comfortable dealing with Christ by proxy than facing Him alone by yourself. It is ever so much easier.

But do you remember the cry which again and again in the Gospels was on Jesus' lips when there was a needy soul to be saved? 'Bring him hither to Me!' Not, mark you, bring him to My disciples, not bring him to the creed-makers, not even bring him to the Church, but — 'Bring him hither to *Me*!' And I think that Paul, if he could see us taking our religion ready-made and accepting other men's beliefs and phrases as our own, would want to cry again, as once he cried to the Corinthians, 'The light of the knowledge of the glory of God is' — where? In your dusty books, your neatly tabulated articles, your controversial documents? No! The light of the knowledge of the glory of God is 'on the face of Jesus Christ', which means that the only way to know anything about God is to go and see Jesus for yourself. Walt Whitman was listening one night to an astronomer lecturing on the stars, and the hall was stuffy, and the lecture dull, and the charts and diagrams unilluminating, until, says Whitman, I could bear it no longer, and I rose and wandered out into the night and looked up at the stars themselves! But there are souls today — thousands of them — who have never thought of doing that, but stay inside poring over the charts and diagrams of religion, the mere mechanism of the faith, taking the whole thing second-hand and quite content with that. 'Men,' cries this New Testament, 'come forth, in the name of God, out of those stuffy places, and look up with your own eyes, and see the bright morning star!'

Again and again this Book drives it home to us that unless our religion is our own it is dead. 'I know whom I have believed,' cries Paul, and sets that down as an impregnable rock in the midst of the swirling waves of the world's doubt — 'I know!' And Peter in his epistle breaks out hotly, 'It is no cunningly devised fable we are giving you, for we were eye-witnesses of Christ's majesty.' Best of all, there is St. John. 'This thing that we are declaring unto you,' he writes in the great opening sentence of his letter, 'this Word of life — we heard it, saw, and gazed upon it, yes, our own hands handled it!' There, he cries, are our credentials — eyes that have gazed into the eyes of Jesus, ears that have known the music of His blessed voice, hands, why, this hand of mine that you see here has clasped again and again the Hand that was pierced! Always it is a personal, immediate experience of Christ on which these men build their case.

And we want that too, don't we? There are three reasons why no sincere soul can rest satisfied with a second-hand religion.

One is that there is always something *unreal* about a religion like that. You are repeating other men's words, and they don't ring true. You sing a hymn like

> 'Jesus, Lover of my soul,
> Let me to Thy bosom fly,'

and the rapture of it and the emotion make you vaguely uncomfortable. Voltaire was one day walking in Paris with a friend, when a religious procession passed them, carrying a crucifix, and Voltaire lifted his hat. 'What?' said his friend, amazed. 'Have you, too, found God?' 'Ah,' said Voltaire sadly and a little bitterly, 'we salute, but we do not speak.' Is not a good deal of present-day religion of that kind — men saluting the cross but not speaking, acknowledging

T–C

God's Christ but having no personal relationship with Him? That is one reason why no sincere soul can be satisfied with a second-hand religion — it is unreal.

Another reason is that it is *insecure*. If it is not your own, it is always at the mercy of doubts. It is always liable to go to pieces on the hard facts of life. Tennyson indeed tells us that whenever his faith was assailed

> 'A warmth within the breast would melt
>   The freezing reason's colder part,
>   And like a man in wrath the heart
> Stood up and answer'd "I have felt."'

But what if that 'warmth within the breast' can't be counted on? Then the doubts have free course to go smashing their way right through! John Wesley had always thought he was a true Christian, until one day his ship was caught in a storm in the Atlantic and fear got hold of him. The only people on board, he noticed, who were not terror-stricken were a little group of Moravian missionaries. And when the storm abated, 'Were you not afraid?' Wesley asked one of them. 'Afraid?' said the Moravian. 'Why should I be afraid? I know Christ!' And then looking at Wesley with disconcerting frankness, 'Do *you* know Christ?' he asked. And at that Wesley for the first time in his life realised that he did not. When it comes to the day of trouble, a second-hand religion is always insecure.

Here is the third reason why no sincere soul can be satisfied with a religion like that: it is *incomplete*. It always gives you the sense of something lacking. You think of the men who obviously have lived by the power of a vital experience of God in Christ — how different they are, how radiant and sure, how unselfish and self-controlled and kingly! Why cannot we all learn their secret? Thomas Hardy one winter evening was walking in the fields, and the world

was bleak and grey and shivery and dismal and dead, everything, his own heart included, wrapped in gloom; when
suddenly from a tree above his head a thrush burst into song,
a veritable carol of joy — and the poet stood still wondering.

> 'I could think there trembled through
>   His happy good-night air
> Some blessed Hope, whereof he knew
>   And I was unaware.'

Is not that how the men who have really seen Christ strike
you, that they have discovered something which we perhaps
are outside of still:

> 'Some blessed Hope, whereof they know
>   And we are unaware'?

Why can't we share it? When Goethe was in his teens, he
stumbled on one of the great hours of life. He discovered
Shakespeare, came upon that glory of music and art. 'I was
one born blind,' he declared, 'who had suddenly been made
to see! I rushed out into the open air, and felt as though for
the first time I had hands and feet.' Would it not be a great
thing some day to stumble on Christ like that? 'All the best
part of experience,' wrote that fine spirit, C. E. Montague,
'consists in discovering that perfectly trite pieces of observa-
tion are shiningly and exhilaratingly true.' Think of our
trite religious beliefs, the things that seem to us nowadays
almost platitudinous, which we can hear and repeat without
the faintest ghost of a thrill — true, yes, we accept them as
true. But 'shiningly and exhilaratingly true' — that is what
we need! Why, it would be like the picture that Robert
Bridges in *The Testament of Beauty* has given us — a room
in a museum and the fossils on the shelves suddenly coming
to life, a winter rose-bed in a garden 'bursting into crowded

holiday of scent and bloom'! It would be like Thomas Chalmers in the manse of Kilmany, quite content to preach for years a cold, dry, formal religion — until one day the south winds of God blew upon his own heart, and from that hour he preached to save. 'Mathematician as I was,' he said, 'I had forgotten two magnitudes — the shortness of time and the vastness of eternity'; but Christ gripped him, and the dead gospel came alive — it had hands and feet now, and a heart throbbing like the heart of Jesus. 'I had heard of Thee,' cries Job, 'with the hearing of the ear, but now mine eye seeth Thee.' And there is an old psalmist who breaks out, 'O God, Thou art *my* God!' What would we not give for a first-hand religion like that?

So we come finally to the practical question. How are we to get it? Jowett of Balliol indeed said we ought not to hope for it. We cannot, he said, 'feel such an attachment to Christ as is prescribed by Thomas à Kempis'. We cannot 'concentrate our thoughts upon a person scarcely known to us, who lived eighteen hundred years ago'. Jowett was never so wide of the mark as then.

But one thing is certain. Everyone of us in this matter must stand alone. Even the saints cannot help beyond a certain point. They have tried again and again to pass on their experience to others, to describe just what they have seen and felt in Christ; but always they come back to this, that the thing (as Paul puts it) is 'unspeakable', it beats them, they just can't get it across. Browning in *Rabbi ben Ezra* speaks of

> 'Thoughts hardly to be packed
>   Into a narrow act,
> Fancies that broke through language and escaped.'

That is the experience of the saints in trying to tell what they have found in Jesus. 'We are just young children,' said

Luther, describing the preachers of the Reformation, 'children learning to speak: we can only use half-words and quarter-words.' And St. Bernard in his great hymn, after trying to tell us about it, throws down his pen at last in dismay:

> 'Ah, this,
> Nor tongue nor pen can show;
> The love of Jesus, what it is
> None but His loved ones know.'

It is as if you asked a man, What is a rainbow? and he replied with a complicated equation about the laws of the refraction of light. That a rainbow! What about the magic and glory of the thing, the ethereal wonder and poetry of it that make it a bridge for the angels? The apostle Paul in F. W. H. Myers's great poem, after trying to tell men about Christ, breaks out desperately:

> 'Oh, could I tell ye surely would believe it!
> Oh, could I only say what I have seen!
> How should I tell or how can ye receive it,
> How, till He bringeth you where I have been?'

That is the heart of it: we shall never know till we have been where Paul has been, and stood where John has stood, and knelt where Mary Magdalene has knelt.

That is why there rings out again and again from these pages a cry, 'Come and see!' 'Simon,' cried Andrew, breaking in on his brother one morning, 'I've found the Christ I've found Him! I don't ask you to take it on my word — but come! Come and see!' And he took his brother's arm and led him to Jesus. The market-place at Samaria was drowsing one summer afternoon in the sun, and the groups round the stalls were idle, when suddenly an excited, dishevelled creature came running down the road from the well.

'Come,' she said, 'see a man that told me all I ever did — is not this the Christ?' And, wondering greatly and half-doubting, they went. But that night when they were back they said to her, 'Now we believe, not because you told us: for we have heard and seen Him ourselves, and know that this is the Saviour of the world!' Yes, somehow we have to get where Andrew was, and Peter, and those Samaritans — as near Christ as that.

But how? I don't know how it is ever to be done except by obeying three simple maxims.

The first is — *keep following*. You say you have never really touched Christ yet, never really looked into His eyes. Ah, but at least you do know the road He is travelling on! Well, keep to that. Surrender your will to His moral ideal: for whatever else may be dark in your religion, this at least is clear, that the purity Jesus stands for, the honour, the manliness, the love, all that is far more worth having than any of the allurements of the world. Get your feet on to that road, for it is down that road somewhere that Jesus is always to be found, and no one who has sought Him there has ever failed to find Him. Therefore, keep following.

The second rule is — *keep praying*. Often men tell you they do not pray because Christ is not real to them: the truth of the matter is, Christ is not real to them because they do not pray. To the man who never prays, God in Christ cannot make Himself real. To the soul which will never subdue its noisy clamour to silence, to listen for the divine voice which guides and blesses and reassures, there is little hope that a convincing religious experience will ever come. But to the man who prays habitually (not only when he feels like it — that is one of the snares of religion — but also when he does not feel like it, in the dry and barren seasons) to the man who keeps praying then, Christ is sure to make Himself real, sure to become the biggest fact in life, filling the whole horizon. How do I know? It is guaranteed on the word of Christ Himself. For listen. 'If any man open the door, I will come in to him.' It is prayer that unlocks the door. And, says Jesus, I will come in! I promise it. There are souls today who are eager to pass from hearsay to experience, eager to see Christ for themselves. But is that door unlocked? Has prayer swung it wide? What about starting to pull the bolts back now? They may be stiff and rusty through long disuse, but still, if you really mean it, they will move. And then the door will be open — and then — why, then, 'even so, come, Lord Jesus!'

Finally, there is this — *keep loving*. For if love is the most Christlike thing in the world, and if you love someone with all your being, does it not follow that Christ cannot be far away? If you have begun to realise that the ultimate meaning of life is love, and if you are allowing a spirit of affection and compassion to banish hardness and censoriousness from your heart, must you not be nearer than you think to Him who was the greatest Lover of all, and to the God who so loved the world that Jesus was His gift?

Perhaps some of us here have been looking for an experience of God in Christ in the wrong place. Perhaps with our intricate doctrines and complicated standards, we have not been nearly simple enough. The greatest simplification of religion ever made was made by Christianity: 'Love is of God; and everyone that loveth is born of God, and knoweth God.' If that does not mean that love is the royal road to a convincing religious experience, I do not know what it means.

How it makes havoc of our narrow dogmatisms and exclusive, man-made orthodoxies! 'Everyone that loveth is born of God.' Will you try to realise that? That every experience of love is already an experience of God? That 'inasmuch as ye have done it unto one of the least of these, ye have done it unto Christ'? That it is not outside your friendships, but precisely *in* them, that Christ comes close, and may be found? That the love you have seen shining in someone's eyes and on some dear human face is actually God's love in Christ for you? That 'he that dwelleth in love dwelleth in God, and God in him', and that therefore Christ is there, an intimate personal possession?

Such is the high road to a first-hand, vital religion. Keep following, praying, loving. And when you call Him Saviour, Lord, and King, you will not be repeating what others have told you. You will be saying it of yourself. And so shall all things be made new.

VII

O Man Greatly Beloved!

'O man greatly beloved, fear not: peace be unto thee,
be strong, yea, be strong. And when he had spoken unto
me, I was strengthened.' — DAN. x. 19.

NO BRANCH OF LITERATURE, IN THE WHOLE RANGE OF
published works, is more fascinating than biography. And no
page in a biography is of more absorbing interest than that
which records some spiritual crisis in the life which is being
described.

The reason for this fascination is not far to seek. It is this,
that on the lesser scale of our own little life we encounter
the same crises ourselves. We, too, in our small way, have to
grapple with success and failure. We, too, must learn how
to manage victory and defeat and happiness and pain. We,
too, have to adjust ourselves to love, or to the lack of it. We,
too, encounter death at the last. All these things — which
are the raw materials of religious experience and spiritual
crisis — are here in the structure of the life which we have
been given to live; and it is intensely interesting to see how
men and women so much greater than ourselves met and
reacted to them. This is the fascination of biography, and of
those pages in it in particular.

Now here in Daniel is such a page. Here is an excerpt
from real life, telling of a profoundly moving spiritual
crisis. Here was a man who turned a corner of the road of
life one day and came upon a new vision of God.

Emerson said that the greatest hour in a man's life is when
he turns the corner of a street and meets a new thought or

impulse or idea. But just think — how supremely great the hour, if that new idea is the living God Himself!

> 'In my soul one hope forever sings,
> That at the next white corner of a road
> My eye may look on Him.'

That is what had happened to Daniel here: he had turned a corner on life's pilgrimage — and there, in front of him, was God!

Is that just fancy, think you? Not at all. It is common experience. If ever you have been moved, in some great hour of the fulfilment of heart's desire, to kneel and pray and offer thanks; if ever, when some hope of years lay ruined, there spoke a still small voice, to steady and control, to lift you from the dust and set you on your feet again, if ever temptation leapt, swift and unheralded, and the edge of the precipice was near, and for a moment your soul was in the balance, and then there came a protecting hand that gripped you just in time and led you back to safety; if ever a word in hymn, or prayer, or sermon has been to you the opening of a window towards Jerusalem; if ever a memory of home, or someone's trust and affection, or the eyes of a little child, or some strange thoughts of a green hill far away and a cross against the skyline, have held honour securely upon the throne of your life in a day when honour was threatened; if ever, amid the clamour of doubt and argument and scepticism, your inmost being has dared to stand and cry, 'I know'; if ever there has fallen across your path some gleam of a light that never was on sea or land — then, I beg you, give that experience its due name. Call it fancy and imagination, and you will be disastrously mistaken. Call it the revelation of God, and you will be gloriously right!

Such is our earthly pilgrimage. You round a bend in the

road, and run into a new idea. You turn a corner on life's ordinary way, and there is the vision of God!

But now come back to Daniel. I ask you to notice this: it was not by any random chance that his great hour came to him. It came as a definite answer to a deliberate quest on the part of the man himself. Look at verse twelve. 'From the first day that thou didst set thine heart to understand, and to chasten thyself before thy God, thy words were heard.' That is what the vision said. What does it tell me? It tells me that if I want a vital religion, if I am sincerely desiring a vivid experience of God, I must not sit down passively, hoping that somehow something will happen to me some day. I must take action. I must discipline my life for it. I must make time for prayer. And here is God's assurance: from the moment when I begin to do that, from the hour in which I set my heart to this, my words will be heard, and a vital experience of God will be on the way.

I knew a medical student once who was troubled about religion. He came to me and said that the whole business of religion seemed to him totally unreal. I asked him if he had tried the way of prayer. 'No,' he said, 'for how can I pray when I'm not sure if there is any God to pray to? It would just be shamming!' I suggested to him that if he honestly felt he could not pray, could not talk to a God whose existence he doubted, he was at least morally bound to give that God — supposing that He existed — a chance to talk to *him*; and that therefore, instead of saying a prayer in the morning and the evening, he should just kneel down, and not say anything, but simply wait quite quietly, and see if God — supposing there were a God — would speak, or reveal Himself in any way. He went away and tried it. Some weeks later I saw him again He told me it had worked. He had found God. Or rather, as he put it, he had not found God — for God had found him. I am sure that no man need lack a convincing religious experience if only he will give some time to it, and discipline himself, and prepare the way for the Lord. From the first day thou didst set thine heart to this thing, God's answer was assured.

Coming back to Daniel's experience, we notice next what was the immediate reaction upon the man himself of this sudden encounter with God. It was an overwhelming sense of personal unworthiness. Look at verse eight. 'I was left alone, and saw this great vision, and there remained no strength in me: for my comeliness was turned in me into corruption.' The first result of seeing God is utter humiliation.

That is inevitable. If I am self-approving and complacent; if I have never yielded up that central citadel in which the natural man takes refuge, the citadel of pride; if I am apt to stand upon my dignity, not deigning to speak a word that might remove misunderstanding; if I imagine that I have any goodness or grace which entitles me to judge or criticise another soul — then that spirit is going to receive a terrible shock when, in some hour of real experience, I meet God face to face! The first reaction of a real religious experience is quite devastatingly humiliating.

Isaiah, the gay and debonair young courtier, met God in the temple, and next moment he was crying, 'Woe is me! I am a man of unclean lips.' Saul of Tarsus, the correct and consciously immaculate Pharisee who had kept the whole law unbroken, met God on the Damascus road, and fell on his face, abashed and utterly ashamed. Simon Peter, the decent, hard-working fisherman, met God in the mists of the morning; and there in his boat he flung himself at Jesus' feet, exclaiming, 'Depart from me, for I am a sinful man, O Lord.' Daniel met God, and immediately — 'There remained no strength in me, and my comeliness was turned into corruption.' And when you and I meet God!

'O how shall I, whose native sphere
  Is dark, whose mind is dim,
Before the Ineffable appear,
And on my naked spirit bear
The uncreated beam?'

For to see God is to see — perhaps for the first time —
yourself. And then, if never before, there breaks the cry.
'God be merciful to me a sinner!'

Was it not so in the days of Galilee? The first feeling which
came to the man or the woman who encountered Jesus was
one of desperate shame. Those clear, steady eyes saw
everything — the little insincerities, the selfishnesses, the
impure thoughts, the social shams, the craven criticisms
made in others' absence, the motives unconfessed. His clean,
strong character made theirs seem dingy by comparison. If
any of them did come to Jesus with heads held high in
conscious righteousness, they were scarce five minutes in
that presence before their eyes fell and they were gazing at
the ground. And do our defences not crumble around us
still, when it is Christ with whom we are dealing? To see our
inmost, hidden thoughts, our flashes of irritated temper, our
way of growing fretted when the days are rushed, in the light
of Jesus with His perfect poise and balance and control; to
see our poor limited affections, and hasty judgments, and
inability to understand one another, in the light of His
amazing love and sympathy; to see our secret tamperings
with temptation in the light of His matchless honour and
dazzling purity — that is utterly devastating to a soul's
high opinion of itself. 'Woe is me, for I am undone; for
mine eyes have seen the King.'

Come back to Daniel and his experience. That overwhelming sense of personal unworthiness was his first reaction. But God led him beyond that. God always does.

Listen to the first words he heard God speak. Look at verse eleven. 'And he said unto me, O Daniel, a man greatly beloved!' — that is, greatly beloved *by God*. And again in verse nineteen: 'O man greatly beloved, fear not.'

How that changes everything! To know that somebody loves you, that someone knowing you exactly as you are, and knowing everything that may ever have happened in your life, can and does most truly love you — that, even on the human level, can change life forever. Have you never seen a lad, growing up to manhood feckless and unreliable and unstable, and then quite suddenly lifting his head and pulling himself together and marching on through life with a new step, becoming a real man, and all because somebody — someone good, and loving, and of the right kind — had come into his life? Yes, even in the most unlikely places, the touch of love works miracles.

> 'If I were damned in body and soul,
>   Mother o' mine, mother o' mine,
> I know whose prayers would make me whole,
>   Mother o' mine, mother o' mine.'

How much more the love of the eternal Father!

And so the revelation came to Daniel here. 'O man greatly beloved' — because beloved of God!

'But what has all this to do with me?' you say. 'I don't see where I come into this.' You do come into it. This is God's word to you. How do I know? Because I have seen it embodied and lived out in Jesus.

Nobody thought Zacchæus very lovable — but Jesus did. No one found a Matthew or a Martha or a Thomas in the least attractive or prepossessing: very ordinary, very feature-less personalities they seemed, with no distinctive talents or social gifts or clever conversation, with really nothing engaging or fascinating about them at all. But Jesus found them amazingly lovable, and yearned to get past mere acquaintanceship to genuine intimacy. And no one did it surprise more than these lonely people themselves. 'What can He possibly see in me?' they wondered, when Jesus looked at them with such affection. They did not know. But sons and daughters of God were what Jesus saw; and seeing that, how could He help but love them?

And that made the whole world new. Out of those depths of shame, to which their first sight of Christ had cast them, they rose and stormed the heights. Hope sprang to birth; and knowing that He thus trusted and believed in them, they felt suddenly able for anything. In those eyes of Jesus, so marvellously understanding, so divinely reassuring, they beheld God. And that was their redemption.

'O man, O woman, greatly beloved' — because beloved by God! If only I could help one doubting soul to see that, no matter how difficult and lonely life may be, this is really true! If only I could send one sad heart out of this church with these words ringing and echoing like a triumph-song! Here is wealth for you more than all the money in the Bank of England, friendship to turn the greyest winter days to summer loveliness — if only you will take it, and walk in the joy and sunshine of it, O soul greatly beloved!

> 'Come down, O Love Divine,
> Seek Thou this soul of mine,
> And visit it with Thine own ardour glowing;
> O Comforter, draw near,
> Within my heart appear,
> And kindle it, Thy holy flame bestowing.'

But now, ere we close, come back to Daniel just once again, and notice finally this: a genuine experience of God has always certain distinguishing marks by which you can recognise it, characteristic effects which it produces in a

man's life. Look at the words of the vision. 'O man beloved,
fear not; peace be unto thee; be strong, yea, be strong.'
There are the three results of getting to know God.

The first is Courage. 'Fear not!' Today the world is full
of people living far below their best, and functioning far
beneath their true level of efficiency, and the major cause of
it is just fear — fear of the unknown, fear of the future, fear
of ill-health, fear of the world's opinion, fear of being left on
the shelf, fear of growing old, fear of death. These phobias,
as the psychologists call them, are everywhere today; and
multitudes of people who are quite unconscious of it, and
would indignantly repudiate the suggestion that they are
afraid, are nevertheless in the grip of them.

But when I listen to a psalmist crying, 'Though the earth
be removed, and though the mountains be carried into the
midst of the sea, we will not fear'; or when I hear a Richard
Baxter exclaiming to the persecutors of his day, 'You can
shut us up in prisons, and shut us out of your church and
kingdom, but shut us out of heaven if you can — you can
kill our bodies, but try whether you can reach our souls';
or when I go into the wards of an Infirmary, and see a man
who knows that the frightful pain he is suffering can never
now be cured, who yet, knowing it, is smiling and steady-
eyed and fearless, then my heart tells me — there are men
who have discovered God!

And if you in your own way have made that great discovery, if you know that your soul by God is greatly beloved,
what is there left to fear? If God be for us, who can be
against us? Certainly not life, cried the apostle, and certainly not death! You are more than conqueror in your
courage.

The second result of knowing God is Peace. 'O man
beloved, fear not: peace be unto thee.' What a devouring
thing worry is! There are few people who get through the
world without suffering at one time or another from this

commonest of all the maladies of the soul. 'Worry,' said William James the psychologist, 'means always and invariably loss of effective power.' We feel inadequate to some situation confronting us: and then life grows fevered, and tempers are short, and nerves upset, and our bustling souls are jaded and fatigued. Quietness and confidence take wings and fly away. Interior peace has simply vanished. Who does not know about this?

I should love to be able to reassure even one or two who may be facing this problem of worry in their own life now that there is a way out into absolute release and freedom. Think of the serenity of Jesus. If anyone ever had good reason for being troubled, He had. Remember the crowded days, the fierce and angry oppositions, the awful toll levied on heart and mind and spirit, the loss of friends, the loneliness, the heartbreak of rejected love— 'O Christ, what burdens bowed Thy head!' Yet in the deep places, no fret nor fever touched Him. Was not His Father with Him? 'Thou wilt keep him in perfect peace, whose mind is stayed on Thee.'

Now that can mean you — if you will receive it. Why worry, when One who loves you is in control? Where God comes, an army with banners marches in to garrison the citadel. God's fellowship is peace.

The third mark, the final distinguishing characteristic, of the life that has found God is Power. 'O man beloved, fear not: peace be unto thee; be strong yea, be strong.' And this is the heart of religion — not an intellectual discovery, but an experience of power; not something that we achieve, but something God puts into us.

Ask Simon Peter how he was able to shake himself free from his weaknesses and to go out and change the world; and he will answer, 'It was not myself, it was nothing at all in me — it was God!' Ask Mary Slessor how she succeeded in transforming a vast district of Africa, and she will tell you

— 'It was not Mary Slessor. She was a poor mill-girl, so timid that she could not cross a Glasgow street. No, it was never she — it was God.'

To know God is courage, and it is peace; but above all, it is power. And I thank God that when I have bungled things and been defeated and made a sorry failure of my hopes, Christ does not come to me and say, 'You must try again! You must try harder, you must try as hard as ever you can' — for there would be no gospel in that, and it would only drive me deeper to despair. But Christ's word is, 'Get closer to God, and He will do it for you! Come closer to Me, and my strength shall be yours.'

And it does work out. I know it. I cannot guarantee that Jesus will make life all roses and honeysuckle and blue skies to anyone who takes His way — I do not think He will. But I can guarantee that, whatever days of darkness or of danger may befall, He will reinforce you inwardly to meet them, and His power will carry you through.

'O man greatly beloved, fear not; peace be unto thee; be strong, yea, be strong!'

> 'His might thy heart shall strengthen,
>   His love thy joy increase;
> Mercy thy days shall lengthen;
>   The Lord will give thee peace.'

VIII

The Heroism of Self-Effacement

'He must increase, but I must decrease.' — JOHN iii.
30.

THE LATE VISCOUNT GREY WRITING ONE DAY TO A FRIEND,
described his feelings on escaping to the country after
months of drudgery in London. 'I felt as if having seen the
wide fields and free sky I had looked God in the face and
been refreshed.' Something like that, I think, is the tonic
effect of this text. To come suddenly upon such words, in a
world that is too often stuffy with the stale atmosphere of
self-interest and self-assertion, is like looking God in the
face and being refreshed.

If John the Baptist had never spoken another word in
Scripture but this, it would have marked him down as a saint.
And I want to speak to you about it now, for I am sure there
must be some in this church for whom the great battle of life
is just to bring themselves to say what John here said.

Consider the circumstances. Here was a man who,
judged by any standard you like, had achieved a solid success.
His name was on every lip. He had the crowd in the hollow
of his hand. And then one day Some One else appeared on
the scene — a young Carpenter from Nazareth — and forth-
with the crowd was gone. And John stood and watched
them go, and all he said was — 'He must increase, I must
decrease.' 'He must wax, I must wane.' Only that; but — is
it not magnificent?

For remember the amazing extent of the success which
John had till then enjoyed. Suppose we apply some tests to

it. Shall we apply the test of numbers? The narrative says:
'Then went out to him Jerusalem, and all Judæa, and all the
region round about Jordan.' He did not have to beg them
to come and be evangelised. He did not have to announce
sensational, topical subjects or intriguing themes flavoured
with a dash of current politics. He did not have to advertise
that the services would be brief and bright and hearty, with
a ten-minute sermon, and the rest an orchestra. They were
not cajoled, or bribed, or enticed: they just came — tens of
thousands of them.

Or shall we apply another test — the range of the man's
appeal? Well, look at that motley throng again. There were
soldiers there, says the evangelist, there were publicans, there
were masses of common sinners; but there were also, at the
other end of the scale, Pharisees, that is to say, the leaders of
religious orthodoxy, great names in the theological world,
and (perhaps even more surprising), Sadducees, the scientific
intelligentsia, who had reacted from creed and church-
going into open scepticism — they were all there, swelling
the crowd, and clamouring for the baptism of the remission
of sins. So wide was the range of his appeal.

Or shall we apply one further test — the test of results in
character? Then mark this — it was no cheap meretricious
excitement, John's revival: men were really being converted
for life, turned from darkness to light, and from the power of
Satan to serve the living God. So whatever test we apply —
numbers, range, results — John's movement was a huge
success.

And then this young Nazarene — this Jesus — appeared,
and John's high hour was done.

I can see three things that must have made this a terribly
difficult experience for the Baptist.

For one thing, he had given up everything for his life-
work. He was a homeless dweller in the desert. Comfort,
ease, security, human love, the faces and voices of the

children who might have been his — he had sacrificed all. And now, only failure seemed his reward. 'My God, why hast Thou forsaken me?'

Then again, something told him that the crowd, having gone, had gone for good. He might have consoled himself with the reflection, 'They will come back again, these people. I have only to bide my time, and they will come flocking back.' But something told him that that would never happen. They were gone for good.

Once more, it was not only that the crowd was gone (I do not suppose crowds mattered vitally to him — he was too big a man for that), but it was that his best, most promising friends and disciples had left him and joined Jesus — Andrew and John the beloved disciple amongst them — and he was left alone. It must have been terribly hard, the kind of difficult experience which tests a man to the very roots of his being.

He might have disliked and hated Christ. He might have grudged Him every recruit He made. He might have gone about belittling his rival's achievement. He might have been like the people today who, when others supersede them, or neglect to consult them sufficiently, allow themselves to be torn with jealousy. He might have done all that. Thousands have done it with far less cause. But he stood there, and mastered his own soul, and said — 'He must increase, but I must decrease.' That is heroism.

I am going to ask you — how did John manage it?

He was able to do it, first, *because his life was rooted in God*. If John had not had a background of God at this crisis, I am sure he would have gone to pieces. It is a terrible thing, if you have no background of God, seeing other people getting the prize on which you had set your heart. It is a terrible thing, if there is no background of God, living in a world that sometimes deals out such crushing disappointments of our dreams. It is a terrible thing, if you have no roots in vital religion, trying to keep your pose and equanimity when the heart is just one big restless ache of unsatisfied desire, or when something has happened that has cut you to the very soul. Without some hold on God, life at such times can be hell. But with God — well, I don't say such things will be easy, I would not mock you by suggesting that even for a deeply religious man or woman the sublimation of an unfulfilled desire can ever be an easy process, or that the bearing of a dreadful disappointment does not hurt. To have your roots in God does not make life easy (it is a cheap theology that suggests that), but it does give you a foundation for your feet to stand on while the inevitable fight for your soul is faced; it does give you a strange serenity and peace in the very midst of the fight; it does help you, like Elijah, to get through the hour of storm and fire and whirlwind to the hour of the still small voice. For to have a background of vital religion means this: you have now the certainty that, whatever happens to you in life — and it may be literally anything — there is a most marvellously understanding heart in final control, a heart that understands you better than your own best friend can understand you, better even than you understand yourself; that the struggle, if only you will be faithful in it while it lasts, will one day prove to have had a meaning; and that if you do the noble thing, the difficult thing now, God will never finally let you down. Will you listen to Dr. Edward Wilson, who died with Scott in the Antarctic? 'This I know is God's own truth, that pain and troubles and trials and sorrows and disappointments are either one thing or another. To all who love God they are love tokens from Him. To all who do not love God and do not want to love Him they are merely a nuisance. Every single pain that we feel is known to God because it is the most loving touch of His hand.' To have that as your faith, to have your roots twined round the everlasting rock which is God, is the most steadying thing in the world. It is really the only thing that can adequately equip any man or any woman for the strains and stresses — physical, emotional, and spiritual — of this difficult, puzzling, and sometimes desperately hurting life. That was one secret of John the Baptist's victory — his vital personal religion, his grasp upon the fact of God.

But to proceed. There was another reason why John was able to speak those noble, self-effacing words, 'He must increase, I must decrease,' namely this: *he saw there was something in Jesus which he himself did not possess.* John's preaching had been all sternness and ruggedness and thunder and lightning and denunciation and the fear of hell: but when Jesus preached, men were conscious of a tender and wooing note they had never heard before. John had only one theme — 'Repent! Repent!' — and that was all necessary and good up to a point; but men found it would take them only part of the way — whereas Jesus led them beyond all that, and actually opened up the road to heaven for their wandering feet. But the deepest difference of all was this. John knew that he was just a common sinner like the folk to whom he preached, and that there was always a risk (as Paul was to put it later) that the man who had preached to others might himself finally be a castaway. He knew enough about his own nature and its weaknesses, his own solitary struggles in the dark for his soul, to realise that he, John, stood with all the rest on the sinners' side of the line: but Jesus was definitely on the other. Jesus had no sin about Him. Jesus could lift men up to God, as no John the Baptist ever could, because Jesus alone — in love and perfect purity — stood at God's right hand. So John looked at Christ, and the thoughts came to him — as it must come to every preacher of the gospel today, and every office-bearer of the Church, and everyone who is on the Christian side at all — 'Who am I that I should even try to talk of Him? Who am I that I should be seeking to help others to see God? Who am I to be carrying this terrific responsibility? God pity me — I am not worthy to touch Christ's feet. He must increase, I must decrease.'

I have suggested, then, two reasons why John was able to speak these noble words — one, that his life was rooted in God, the other, that he saw there was something in Jesus which he himself did not possess. There was a third reason, I think, and it was this: John had the grace to see that *it did not matter who did the work, as long as the work was done*. His whole attitude, in effect, was this: Who recks of John the Baptist, if God get the glory? What counts the messenger, if only the message go right home? Let John's name be obliterated forever, if only men be saved, and God the Lord enthroned!

That was his attitude. And there is a great principle here for us: it does not matter who does the work, as long as the work is done. In Whittier's words:

> 'What matter, I or they?
> Mine or another's day,
> So the right word be said,
> And life the sweeter made?'

Or, in the fine watchword of the great Lord Shaftesbury, 'Perish all things, so that Christ be magnified!'

How slow we are to realise this! How often our attitude is, 'It does matter who does the work — it is going to be done by me!' And so Christian service gets mixed up with questions of precedence, and Christian people grow sensitive about these personal things, and Christian love forgets the first essential — which is thorough-going self-effacement.

I repeat — it does not matter who does the work, as long as the work is done. Some religious movements have still to realise this. Some almost hold that no one is truly converted who has not been converted under their auspices. That attitude runs right back to the Early Church. Do you remember Corinth? One sect said, 'We are of Paul'; another, 'We are of Apollos'; another, 'We are of Cephas' — and the implication was, 'If you do not belong to us, you are not the real thing! Only those who have travelled our spiritual road, and have come into the kingdom through our gate, are really in the kingdom at all.' Do you remember Paul's reply? He had to reply to that — it was so dangerously untrue, and so terribly unlike the Spirit of Jesus. 'Is Christ divided?' he said. 'Who is Paul, who is Apollos, who is Cephas, but mere instruments in the hands of God? The instrument is nothing: God is everything.' Would that all religious people could take that to heart! It does not matter how or by whom souls are saved, as long as they are saved. The movement is nothing: Christ is everything. 'Who cares for the Free Church,' said Thomas Chalmers, and he himself was the greatest of Free Churchmen, the founder and the leader of the movement in his land, but 'Who cares for the Free Church,' he cried, 'compared with the Christian good of Scotland?' Who cares for any Church, or denomination, or group, or fellowship, or party — compared with Christ? Get the movement out of sight: magnify Jesus! He must increase, the movement decrease. The movement rises, does its work, and passes away into the limbo of forgotten things: the Christ to whom it points goes on. Widen your horizons! There are others, thank God, working for Christ in totally different ways from yours or mine. There are gates into the kingdom of heaven, says Revelation, from every point of the compass. There are scores of paths up the hill of the Lord. It does not matter who does the work, as long as the work is done.

And this applies to our individual service too. Suppose you are trying to help another soul, some man or some woman who has been finding life tangled and difficult. It may be that, to begin with at any rate, that other soul's hold upon God is bound up with you, and with what it sees of God in you. And so you twine your life round that other life, to help it through the difficult place. But the point is this, that when you have brought that other face to face with Christ (and nothing less can be your ultimate aim), then He will take charge. From that point on, Christ is to increase, you are to decrease. And the question is, When you reach that point, where Christ is really seen, will you have grace to step back? If you are a parent, will you step back and give your child room to develop his or her own personality, not dictating in morals or religion, but leaving that young life to walk its own Emmaus road with Christ? If you are a church worker, will you step back and stand in the shadow that Christ may stand in the light? I know a little church in the Highlands, where the first thing your eye lights on when you enter the vestry is a saying of Denney's, framed upon the wall: 'No man can give at once the impressions that he himself is clever and that Christ is mighty to save.' If you are a friend, trying to help a friend, will you remember that the greatest of all helpers is Jesus, and will you step back, saying, 'Don't look at me, look at Him'? Our Christian service may be diligent and keen and zealous, but it is ruined without self-effacement. And, on the other hand, our service may be unseen, and our very name forgotten; but if one dear soul we love has discovered Christ, the work will have been done. 'He must increase, I must decrease.'

And so we come finally to this — that if these words are to be the motto of our outward service, they must first be the keynote of our inner life. I suppose that in everyone of us at this moment there is something of self, and something of Christ. And what God wills is this, that that bit of self in me, the 'ego' as we call it, the thing which says 'I', 'mine', 'me', is progressively to contract and be superseded; while the other thing, the God principle, is to expand and grow and take

control. He — the indwelling Christ — must increase; and I
— the self — must decrease.

That is an epitome of the Christian life. And I wonder —
what stage have we reached in the process? Is Christ in us
gaining ground? Is self in us retreating from the field? 'He
must increase, I must decrease.' Is it happening?

'O the bitter shame and sorrow,
   That a time could ever be
When I let the Saviour's pity
Plead in vain, and proudly answered,
    "All of self, and none of Thee!"

Yet he found me; I beheld Him
   Bleeding on the accursèd tree,
Heard Him pray, "Forgive them, Father!"
And my wistful heart said faintly,
    "Some of self, and some of Thee!"

Day by day His tender mercy,
   Healing, helping, full, and free,
Sweet and strong, and, ah! so patient,
Brought me lower, while I whispered,
    "Less of self, and more of Thee!"

Higher than the highest heaven,
   Deeper than the deepest sea,
Lord, Thy love at last hath conquered;
Grant me now my supplication,
    "None of self, and all of Thee!"'

IX

Vanguard and Rearguard

'The Lord will go before you; and the God of Israel will be your rereward.' — ISA. lii. 12.

HOW DO YOU REGARD HUMAN LIFE? I SUPPOSE THE THREE most frequent descriptions of life, the three most popular pictures, are these — a battle, a voyage, and a march.

Many have spoken of it as a battle. 'For my own part,' declared William James in a famous passage, 'I do not know what the sweat and blood and tragedy of this life mean, if they mean anything short of this. If this life be not a real fight, in which something is eternally gained for the universe by success, it is no better than a game of private theatricals from which one may withdraw at will. But it *feels* like a real fight.'

And many have spoken of it as a voyage, the passing of a ship across seas which today may be as smooth as glass, and tomorrow tossed with a hurricane — on and on, till the harbour lights appear on the other side and the desired haven is won.

But the picture which doubtless has the widest appeal is that of life as a march. We talk about 'the milestones of the years'. We put our ear to the ground and we hear the tramp, tramp, tramp of the hosts of humanity. We turn the pages of history and we see the calvacade of the sons of men. Life is a march.

Many of the greatest spirits who have ever lived have taught us to regard it so. John Bunyan for one, with his immortal pictures of the road beaten bare by the passing of pilgrim feet. Thomas Carlyle, for another. Some of you will remember the page in *Sartor Resartus*, one of the most glittering, thrilling pages in English literature, where he pictures the generations rising out of darkness into daylight, each living out its brief enthralling day, and then plunging back into the dark again, each (as he puts it) 'hasting stormfully across the astonished earth,' each leaving 'on the hardest adamant some footprint stamped in,' so that 'the last rear of the host will read traces of the earliest van.' You have it again in Matthew Arnold, in that glorious poem, *Rugby Chapel* — the picture of mankind marching in one vast, interminable column across the face of the ages, many of them dispirited, but still the march going on, and still the column pressing forward:

> 'On, to the bound of the waste,
>   On, to the City of God.'

And you have it in many of the greatest hymns of the Church, those songs we sing together to rally the courage in the depths of our souls:

> 'Through the night of doubt and sorrow
>   Onward goes the pilgrim band,
> Singing songs of expectation,
>   Marching to the promised land.'

That is the history of the sons of men. That is our own life today — with the milestones hurrying by.

And that is Isaiah's picture here. Only — mark this — he has added something to it. He has added something most dramatically important. Carlyle spoke of the last rear of the host reading traces of the earliest vanguard. Isaiah has a far more glorious vision than Carlyle. 'That vanguard on in front,' he says, 'that is *God* — God at the head of the host

— the spearhead of humanity's advance! That rearguard following after,' he continues, 'that too, is *God*, God coming up behind, God holding the post of danger at the army's rear!' That is Isaiah's vision — 'Onward goes the pilgrim band,' with God in front, and God behind, and your marching soul in the midst, encircled by God, barricaded in by God, surrounded by God as by a wall of steel and iron. And that is the promise which rings out deathlessly to cheer us on our way: 'The Lord will go before you; and the God of Israel will be your rearguard.'

The Lord our vanguard! Has not that been your experience on the road? Can't you look back today and put your finger on place after place and say, 'Here, and here, and here I was 'to grace how great a debtor' — here and there God had prepared the way for me'?

Take the longest view. Look back on the whole course of your life. Has not God always been beforehand with you? And if you love Him today, is it not because — as St. John puts it with great simplicity — He has always loved you first?

Think of the surprises that His grace has so often brought to you. At birthdays and Christmas seasons you prepare surprises for the children and those you love. You smuggle things into the house. You keep them locked away. You guard your secret well. And then, when the happy morning comes, you bring out the thing you have prepared, a glad, loving surprise. Is not that what the great Father of heaven does times without number for His children? And is not half the magic of life just this, that it is so full of the thrill of discovery — and all because a God of love is going on before?

Or turn from the joys you have had, and think of the sorrows. Think of the frustrations, the griefs, the disappointments, the pathos of shattered dreams; and see if you cannot

say, looking back now, that even in those experiences grace
was present, even there God was leading on, with a definite
plan for your life.

There is an historic incident from the story of Oliver
Cromwell and John Hampden, those two stalwart makers of
England. It was in the days when they were still almost
unknown. So utterly weary and impatient had they grown
of the way in which king and court and government were
ruining the nation and bringing it down to decadence and
disaster that they decided there was only one course left for
them to take, and that was to leave the country and never
set foot in it again. Memories of the *Mayflower's* intrepid
adventure kept urging them, and their thoughts turned
longingly to the new colony beyond the seas where the winds
of freedom blew and life was clean. One day news came to
them that a ship lying in the Thames was shortly to make
the Atlantic crossing. Quietly and unobtrusively Cromwell
and Hampden took their places on board. Everything was in
readiness for the long voyage; the two men had shaken from
their feet the dust of the land whose downfall they lamented,
when, at the last moment, messengers dashed up with orders
from the king that on no account were they to be allowed to
sail. Baulked and frustrated and angry at their fate, Cromwell and Hampden came ashore: it was the ruin of their
hope. But it was that ruin that gave Cromwell to England,
and shaped the subsequent course of history. Had not God,
even in the wreck of the man's plans, been going on in
front?

And can you not say the same of sorrows that have
marked your way — things, perhaps, that once came
near making you ready to 'curse God and die'? And yet
today:

> 'I'll bless the hand that guided,
> I'll bless the heart that planned!'

'We love Him, because He first loved us.' He has always been first. He has been 'the Lord our vanguard.'

And therefore (this is the point we have been making for), a brave heart to the passing milestones — greet the unseen with a cheer!

We talk about 'the unknown future'; we say timidly that we have no notion whatever of what may be coming to us. It is not true! 'But surely,' protests someone, 'It *is* true. We can't tell what a day may bring forth; we don't know one single thing about what may be on there in front.' I say again, It is not true. One thing I know, *God* is on there in front! One thing I can say, Whatever that future is going to bring forth, it is going to bring us God. *The Lord our vanguard — that* I know. And is not that enough?

That brave, shining light of the Church of England, Studdert Kennedy, in the last book he wrote before his death, a book called *The Warrior, the Woman, and the Christ*, described the moment when real religion was first born within him. He was alone at night on a moor beside the sea. Above him was the great black dome of heaven, and a million stars. There was no sound but the boom of the waves against the cliff. He was alone; and yet he was acutely conscious of a great, vast, mysterious presence — the spirit of the universe — moving there in the dark. He felt that night as he was to feel on another later occasion, when he lay by himself in no man's land between the trenches and watched a moving figure coming towards him, not knowing whether it were friend or foe. Suppose he whispered, 'Who goes there?' Would the answer be a bullet, or a friendly word, or silence? Just so he had felt on this night alone on the moor beside the sea. Suppose he cried out to that mysterious spirit of the universe, 'Who goes there?' Would there be any answer? Or would there be nothing but the boom of the waves, and the whisper of the wind in the heather? He decided to risk it. He made his cry, 'Who goes there?' And in that very moment his soul received an answer. And the answer was one word — God. And from that hour he knew, and believed.

Here are we today, with the dark mystery of the veiled future confronting us, wondering (as it is perfectly natural to wonder) what is moving there for us behind the veil, joy or sorrow, friend or foe, success or failure, life or death. But if you stand today, and cry into that black mysterious void, 'Who goes there?' — you will get your answer. 'God goes there! Love goes there. Your Father is there!' And again I ask you, Is not that enough?

'The Lord will go before you' — whatever else is hidden, that is gloriously certain. God our vanguard!

But glorious as it is, that does not finish Isaiah's picture of the march. With sudden, dramatic imagination he has added this — 'and the God of Israel will be your rereward.'

It is almost certain that here the prophet had the story of the Exodus in mind. Israel had escaped from Egypt; across the open desert the angel of God was leading them; the pillars of cloud and fire were going on before: when suddenly from the rear of the marching host a terrible cry was raised, 'The Egyptians! We are pursued! Egypt is on our track!' Yonder on the southern horizon was the cloud of dust, where Pharaoh's chariots and horses were steadily drawing nearer. Again the cry was raised, 'The destroyer is after us! He is gaining ground. What shall we do?' And then comes the most wonderful touch in the story. 'The angel of God, which went before the camp of Israel, removed and went behind them; and the pillar of cloud went from before their face, and stood behind them.' Is it not a glorious picture — God coming in to hold the rear and fight the rearguard action, God Himself coming down like a great divine barrage that the destroyer could not pass?

Do you see the parable for us? 'The God of Israel will be your rearguard.' For if the Christian life is an onward march, it is also a rearguard action. Old forsaken things, whose bondage we thought was broken, come hurrying after. They come so near sometimes that you can feel their hot, foul breath upon your soul — insinuating habits, stubborn temptations, strong, masterful sins.

Has a man, in some high hour of gladness, given Christ his heart? The devil does not take a reverse like that lying down. He does not say, 'I am sorry to lose you — but if your mind is made up, I suppose that settles it. Go with Christ if you must!' Nothing so easy as that. He begins the the pursuit. It may be he will never stop pursuing. Whyte of St. George's was once describing the way in which the blood-hounds of temptation and remorse can sometimes haunt the soul. 'You may be saved,' he cried, 'but they will pursue you up to the very gates of heaven, and leave the bloody slaver of their jaws upon the golden bars!'

The soul's enemies pursue. And sometimes (God forgive us) we almost want to desert, and go over to that pursuing foe.

But what happens? Just what happened to Israel. 'The angel of God, that went before the camp' — give that angel his right name now — 'the Christ of God, who went before, removed and went behind.' The Lord our rearguard!

And can't you see Him — Christ, with the sword of His Spirit, holding the rear of our march, barring the way of our hereditary foes, delivering us from the menace of their onset, defending us from the even worse disaster of desertion? Where would any of us have been today if Christ had not been our rearguard?

'But', as John Bunyan put it, in one swift, poignant phrase, 'not without great danger to Himself — which made me love Him the more.' I am going to end now by reminding you of what it has cost God to keep the rear of our onward march, and of the terrible price of that rearguard action to Jesus.

There was an hour — a grey, grim, terrible hour — when Napoleon in Russia, finding Moscow burnt before him, and his supplies fast running out, faced round westward to begin the long retreat to Paris. He summoned the man he could count on best, the brave, gallant Marshal Ney. 'I appoint you, my Marshal,' he said, 'to command the rearguard. You are to keep the Russians back from the main body of my army. You are to be the breakwater between us and the deluge. You are to block their advance at any price, till I extricate my men from this trap of death and get them home to France.' And Marshal Ney promised that he would do it. He drew his troops into line and slowly, grimly, they began to fight their way back, taking on themselves the full weight of the Russian march of death, enduring indescribable things from wounds and frost and famine. So the terrible days and nights wore past. And then, it is said, one day long afterwards, when some officers were playing cards in their quarters in Paris, the door of the room opened, and there stood before them the most dishevelled figure they had ever seen, old and bent and emaciated, his clothing tattered, his hands trembling, and lines of terrible suffering carved deep into his features. 'Who are you?' they cried, startled. But suddenly, to one of them, there came a flash of recognition. 'Why', he exclaimed, springing to his feet, 'it's the Marshal! It's Marshal Ney!' And the others rose, and saluted. 'Tell us, Marshal,' they said, when they had conquered their astonishment, 'tell us — for we have been wondering — where *is* the rearguard?' And the bent, broken figure squared his shoulders a moment, and looked them in the face: 'Sirs', he said, '*I am* the rearguard!' And it was a fact. He alone had seen it through.

Who is this that cometh from Edom, with dyed garments from Bozrah, this that is red in His apparel, His garments stained in blood; this whose visage is marred more than any man, and His form more than the sons of men; this from whose head and hands and feet sorrow and love flow mingled down? This is the Christ. '*I am* the rearguard', says Jesus.

And when you think of the onward march of humanity today, and when you think of your own soul's march from the past into the future, remember there is not only a God on in front there, leading the way: remember there is also Something behind, Some one facing backwards down the road you have travelled; and His arms, as He gazes back to the foe, are stretched out wide, wide as the cross of Calvary — wide as the world those arms are stretched, to bar the way. O blessed, suffering, gallant God — Thou art the rearguard!

And, therefore, to any troubled soul here today — and never a congregation meets but troubled souls are there, some of them apprehensive of the future, others worried about the past — the word of God is, Courage! Take heart through Christ, take heart! The past is God's, and the future is God's; and the power of the love of Jesus to hold your spirit strong and steady is really far greater, if you would but believe it, than the power of outward circumstance to violate your peace. Therefore, pilgrim soul, march singing! March with the serenity of Christ possessing you! Past the milestones of the years keep marching — until the long road leads to sunset and evening star and journey's end, and the towers and turrets of the City of God appear beyond the river. God is your vanguard, God your rearguard. Therefore sing — and march!

X

The Fellowship of the Spirit

'The communion of the Holy Ghost be with you all.'
— 2 Cor. xiii. 14.

THE COMMUNION OF THE HOLY GHOST! THE FELLOWSHIP OF
the Spirit! Here is a phrase that leads straight to the core
and centre of the Christian experience.

The first thing we need to get quite clear is that this great
conception, rooted here in St. Paul's Trinitarian benediction,
means two things, not one. For there is no such thing as
fellowship of believers among themselves apart from the
fellowship of the separate souls with God; and there is
no fellowship with God which does not produce as its primary
and characteristic result a living fellowship with men. Now
that lays down the lines for our thoughts to follow. Let us
think first of the Christian fellowship in the world; and
then let us think of the lonely fellowship with God that lies
behind it.

It is an extraordinarily vital and impressive thing — the
Christian fellowship that meets you in the pages of the New
Testament. Here you have Saul of Tarsus, haughty Pharisee,
Hebrew of the Hebrews, who took care that everybody
should know it, sharing his deepest intimacies with poor
illiterate slaves from Greek slums, barbarians, he would
once have called them, Scythians, miserable outsiders —
yet now miraculously his brothers. Only one thing explains
it — Christ. Here you have a Christian love-feast in the
catacombs, and a Roman lady, with imperial blood in her
veins, a kinswoman of the Caesars, taking the cup from the

hand of a nameless waif of the streets, and both of them feeling it was the most natural thing in the world to do, for there was a love deeper than sisterhood between them now. Only one thing explains it — Christ.

It was an amazing thing, that early fellowship; and it meant everything to those who shared it. When they met temptation out in the world — the lust of the flesh, the lust of the eye, and the pride of life — the fellowship was an unseen reinforcing host, backing them up, steadying them, putting them on their honour, giving them victory. Young converts coming into the fellowship out of heathenism found that in the testing days after their conversion, when the first glow had passed and the old environment was trying to drag them down again, it was the fellowship that held them up. Not that these early Christians were always talking about their fellowship. It never occurred to them to make orations about it. And they never tried to organise it in a semi-professional way, saying, 'It is our duty as Christians to be brotherly: let us start a meeting to promote brotherhood.' That would have seemed to them utterly trivial and foolish. Their fellowship was this — that they were sharing together the very life of Jesus. And the trouble with us today is that far too often we have tried to run a superhuman fellowship on a human basis. And it can't be done. We have tried to organise and mechanise and work the thing up, not seeing that the fellowship of the Church is going to be just as limited, just as disruptive, just as much at the mercy of temperament and frail human nature as all the other fellowships of this world — unless it is true to its own supernatural origin, and builds on an experience of Christ.

Now there is one thing I ask you to notice specially about that fellowship of the Spirit in the New Testament, namely this: it never wasted time on mutual admiration, as though the fellowship were an end in itself. It never became esoteric for it was the Body of Christ, existing for Christ's purposes

in the world. It never sang, as alas! its successors of a later
day have sometimes sung:

> 'We are a garden walled around,
>   Chosen and made peculiar ground;
>   A little spot enclosed by grace
>   Out of the world's wide wilderness.'

There was far more of John Masefield's Saul Kane about it:

> 'I knew that Christ had given me birth
>   To brother all the souls on earth.'

Always the fellowship was drawing others to itself. Always it
was self-propagating.

Every member of that early fellowship knew himself to be
a herald. He knew that that was the condition on which
his own place in the fellowship depended. I wonder if we
have ever fully realised that the very life of the fellowship
today depends on each member of it being (to use the
language of electricity) a *Christ-conductor*? 'Your brain,'
an old schoolmaster of Ernest Raymond's used to say to his
class, 'shouldn't be a cold-storage chamber, but a power-
house.' That is even truer of the soul than of the brain. Our
soul is not to be a cold-storage chamber where our personal
religion is stocked and hidden away, but a power-house
sending out into the world the light and warmth and radiance of the Christ. That is what God wants today, not
apologists arguing for Him — God has been argued for long
enough — but heralds proclaiming Him. Thomas Carlyle,
speaking of his *French Revolution*, once said: 'This I could
tell the world: you have not had for a hundred years any
book that comes more direct and flamingly from the heart of
a living man.' That is how our witness as members of the
fellowship ought to come, direct and flaming from the heart.

And even if we cannot tell it out (for Christ is glorious beyond our poor stammering words), we can at least live it out, and so share it with the world. Some time ago, in the *Spectator*, there was a review of a book on the poet Blake, and in the course of it the reviewer said that the cry raised by the world's greatest literature is, 'Read me, do not write about me, do not even talk about me, but read me!' To me it seems that the cry raised by the world's great Christ today is: Live Me, do not debate about Me, do not even argue for Me, but live Me! That, surely, is what the fellowship is meant for — to be out in the world living Christ, scattering the glory, heralding the Lord. And it is the very death of the fellowship if it fails its Master here.

But now we must go deeper. I said at the beginning that the 'fellowship of the Spirit' means two things, not one; and we turn now to the other side. Behind that wonderful Christian fellowship that burned and glowed in the Early Church there lay a direct individual fellowship with God, a personal experience of the Holy Spirit. In other words, behind it was Pentecost.

Now we have been told scores of times in these recent years (and certainly it is true) that to recapture Pentecost is the prime need of the Church today. But I suppose that for many of us the story of Pentecost as it stands in the New Testament, with its record of rushing winds and cloven fires and gifts of tongues, is strange and dark and mysterious; and the big question for many minds is, What was it that really happened there? That something happened, something tremendous and revolutionary and startling and sudden, is clear: and any historian, studying the New Testament, whether he is a Christian or not, freely recognises that on this particular page and on the pages that come after it there rings out in the lives of these followers of Christ a note which had not been there before; that here, in a single moment, the human fumbling and faltering which had so often come between these men and Jesus is all finished; and that from this point you get the throb and the beat of the march of men whose heads are up, who are utterly sure of themselves because they are utterly sure of God. All who give thought to Christian origins (even historians with no particular Christian bias) are agreed that here, at this definite point and on this definite day of history, something happened that saved Christianity for the world. But what was it? What does Pentecost really mean?

I would have you notice two simple but decisive things about the men who got the experience.

They were expectant men. That is to say, Pentecost did not happen in a vacuum. It happened in an atmosphere where faith and eagerness had prepared the way. It came to men who were taking time to *listen* for God.

And there will never be a Pentecost without that — either for the individual or for the Church. We complain sometimes that we have never had much in the way of definite spiritual experience, and perhaps we even come to think that we were not meant for it, that it is 'not in our line'. But with all my heart I believe that God has a great spiritual experience waiting for any man or woman who will rise up to receive it. I do not see how we can believe the New Testament and the Christ of the New Testament, and not believe that. But it is the listless, bored, apathetic, non-expectant attitude that baulks God all along the line. If I say my prayers, for example, as a kind of job I had better put through, if when I go home tonight I finish up the day with a prayer because it is a habit, a custom, nothing more — I am taking the channel between God and myself that Jesus Christ has dug with His own hands, and blocking it. But if I can offer to God a prayer electrically charged with faith, if in the hushed shrine of my secret soul I am really expecting God to speak, listening for that, then God will speak indeed. I

know it, for He has done it. And you know it, for He
has done it for you. It is the expectant heart to which the
Holy Spirit comes.

The other simple but decisive thing about these men who
first got the great experience was this. *They were Christ-
surrendered men.* Every one of them had given himself to
Christ up to the hilt, and was ready to go anywhere, do
anything, at Christ's command.

Is it there our difficulty lies? Let me say this quite clearly:
none of us has a right to complain that God gave these men
of the New Testament a spiritual experience He has never
given us, if we have not gone the lengths with Christ that
they went, have never done what they did, taken the circle
of our life and lifted it up bodily off the centre called self, and
set it down and rooted it on the centre called Jesus. Pentecost is God's answer to a soul's surrender to Jesus: it
comes after the surrender, not before.

That is precisely our trouble. We want God's Spirit,
without God's conditions. How often it happens, for
instance, that when some great moral issue is raised — it
may be in the world at large, some issue like war and peace,
or it may be in our own secret life, where no one knows
anything about it but ourselves — how often it happens that
we argue, and go on arguing, the matter! What we don't do
is to say, 'God has given His orders: that is an end of it.
There is no need for argument!' It is so very much easier to
spend a dozen hours discussing religion than one half-hour
obeying God. It is so pitifully easy to give God a half-
obedience, a second-best religion — not the kind of thing
that that great soul Temple Gairdner was urging when he
said about a certain temptation: 'Take it out into the desert
with Christ and throttle it!'

I am sure that in these recent years we have been con-
tenting ourselves far too much with a merely friendly and
appealing Jesus, instead of a strong, imperial, commanding

Jesus; and with a gospel of good fellowship and camaraderie, instead of a gospel of downright obedience. The real danger of the idea of a semi-dependent Christ, who appeals for help, is that almost inevitably you will have men imagining that by professing Christianity they are doing Christ a favour. You know what is apt to happen whenever any prominent man of letters or man of science writes an article in which he speaks approvingly about Jesus of Nazareth and the Christian religion. Immediately there are crowds of Christians ready to applaud it, as if it were another feather in the cap of Christianity, ready to broadcast it excitedly — 'So-and-so has given his vote for Christianity: isn't it fine?' — as much as to say, 'How gratified Jesus must be!' That is all wrong. It is a travesty of the truth. Christ does not court any man. Christ commands him. And Christianity does not consist in complimenting Christ as genius, or artist, or poet, or teacher, or social reformer, or anything else whatever: it means bowing to Christ as Commander. It is being ready to make His will our law, His command our joy, and His hardest marching-orders the music of our life.

This is the crux of the matter. Pentecost is God's answer to men's obedience to His Son. The Spirit comes to those, and to those alone, who can say to Christ such words as Robert Herrick three hundred years ago said to his Anthea:

'—Thou art my life, my love, my heart,
The very eyes of me,
And hast command of every part,
To live and die for thee.'

To those men of the New Testament, so expectant, so utterly Christ-surrendered, the Spirit came. And the heart of the experience was not the rushing winds, nor the fires, nor the tongues — these were mere accessories and corroborations. The heart of the experience was *power* — a power that shook them to the very depths of their souls, and then sent them out to shake the earth.

It is power that our religion lacks today: not organisation, not intellectual equipment, not social idealism — but power. And there is no secret of power except in a deepened spiritual experience. Such an experience we can have, if — a big 'if' this — we want it with all our heart and soul, and if we are prepared to pay down the price of it in self-surrender to Christ and self-commitment to the holy will of God.

Now that brings us, finally, to this. The fellowship of the Spirit is power on certain different levels. *It is power on the physical level*. Look at the men of the New Testament. Quite apart from their spiritual force, they were physically twice the men they had been before, tingling with an energy and a verve which they themselves formerly would not have believed possible, and carrying things through triumphantly which would once have broken them. For a spiritual experience exhilarates a man's very body. That is not hard to understand. You see, it puts a new song into his heart; and naturally that reacts beneficially upon his nerves, and instincts, and the whole tone and balance of his physical frame, imparting a marvellous degree of peace, and pose, and serenity. Indeed, the idea that to be religious is to have a cramped and weakly life is one of the most stupid heresies ever invented, so stupid as to be mere rubbish. There is a Jewish legend which tells how Satan was once asked what he missed most since he had fallen from his former high estate in heaven. 'I miss most,' he answered, 'the trumpets in the morning!' The Spirit of God keys a man up — like trumpets at dawn — to a pitch of vitality that no worldly spirit knows anything about; and even on the physical level, the fellowship of the Spirit is power.

It is power also on the mental level. It is possible to make far too much of the illiterate character of the Early Church. In point of fact, that Church had in its membership some of the best brains of the ancient world. And what a power of initiative they had, what a sureness of touch, what a keen eye for essentials, what a directness of decision! The world had never seen anything like it. The fellowship of the Spirit is power on the mental level.

It is power on the moral level. Look at those men again. Many of them had spent half a lifetime at the beck and call of devouring, devastating passions; many of them had had wasted, shrivelled, burnt-out souls — until Jesus had got hold of them, and by a miracle of grace had wrenched them clear and set them with their faces to the sky; and now there they were, walking through cities that were living dens of corruption, and yet clad in the purity of Christ! Ask anyone of them how it happened. 'It is not I,' comes the answer, 'but the Spirit of God in me.' What a message of hope today for defeated souls! Do you say your will is powerless? Perhaps it is. But Christ does not say, 'Try harder.' Christ says, 'Accept the power of God.' There is not a temptation on the face of the earth — no matter how dogged and stubborn it may be — which cannot be smashed, if only that same conquering Spirit is given His chance. The fellowship of the Spirit is power on the moral level.

And, above all, *it is power on the spiritual level.* What mighty missionaries the men of Pentecost were! Wherever they went, lives were changed, and souls redeemed. It was not anything they said that did it: it was the way they lived. They had been swept out of all narrowness and pettiness and selfishness and censoriousness and repression into a life that was radiant and released and exultant and contagious; and the world, looking at them could only say, 'You have been with Jesus! You have found the secret. Help us to find it too!'

And that is meant to be normal Christianity. That is the impact your life and mine might be making on the world around us, if we were really men and women of the Spirit.

I put it to you now, as I put it to myself — is there something still impeding that? Something unsubdued to Christ and therefore spoiling all our Christian witness? There was a day in Napoleon's life when disaffection and mutiny had broken out among the men of the Old Guard, and the risk was great. But Napoleon knew how to meet it. He sat alone in a little room in his palace, a room, which had two large apartments opening off it to right and left; and in the hall to the left the members of the Guard were assembled. Each man was summoned alone to Napoleon, and as he entered the door was shut. Not a word was spoken; but Napoleon clasped the man's hand and looked him full in the face. Then each passed out again by the door on the right, until the whole of the Guard, one by one, had passed through. And when all had passed, the disaffection and the mutiny were over. The silent look and the handclasp had done their work: every man of them was Napoleon's now.

Here within this House of God, our Commander Jesus is summoning us to Him, one by one. He is looking us full in the face. His hand, pierced with the nail, is clasping ours. Can we still hold something back? Must we not go out from that silent Presence, His followers unconditionally, His without reserve? So shall we be men and women full of the Spirit of God, and strong in His glorious name.

XI

Anchors of the Soul

'Then fearing lest we should have fallen upon rocks, they cast four anchors out of the stern, and wished for the day.' — ACTS xxvii. 29.

HERE IS A QUESTION THAT IS WORTH ASKING. HAVE YOU AND I any anchors on board the ship? And are they strong enough for the day of storm? Are they fit for the strain of life and death, and joy and terror, and everything that may happen on life's seas?

Some people's faith is purely a fair-weather thing. Some have constructed their religion on the assumption that they are going to meet calm seas and favourable breezes all their voyage through. Some have never taken time or trouble to sit down in the cabin for half an hour with the great Captain, and reckon on the possibilities of gales and rocks and angry, buffeting waves.

It may be, of course, that even so they will get through without trouble. It may be that some tender Providence will hold the storms in leash, and see them safely home to their desired haven. It may be that they will never awake at night with the winds shrieking outside and the wild sea showing its teeth.

But what a dreadful risk! In a world like this, where the wisest cannot tell what a day may bring forth, where without a moment's warning the whole aspect of the skies may be changed, it is surely a risk which no serious man or woman would care to face. And so the question, for you and for me and for every voyaging soul, is — What about the anchors? Are they there?

Here was this ship, labouring against that tempestuous wind Euroclydon, tossed in the wild Mediterranean, threatened by the crags and rocks of Malta; and, says the writer, 'they cast four anchors out of the stern, and wished for the day'. Have you ever done that? Have you ever wished and prayed for the day, when the night was black? There are worse winds in life than Euroclydon, and stormier seas than the Mediterranean, and crueller rocks than Malta — wild winds of doubt, and sorrow's bitter seas, and temptation's jagged rocks: and in amongst them, the frail ship that is a man's soul, battered and benighted and wishing to God for the morning! As Herbert Trench puts it:

'When round thy ship in tempest Hell appears,
    And every spectre mutters up more dire
        To snatch control
    And loose to madness thy deep-kennell'd Fears—
        Then to the helm O Soul!'

It may come. It has come to thousands. It may come one day to you. Is the ship equipped with anchors? Have you enough of them? Are they fit for the strain? Are they anchors that will hold?

'They cast four anchors out.' Let us give the four anchors their names. And let us pray the good God that they may be part of the equipment of us all.

We do not need to search far for the first. There is only one other place in Scripture where the word 'anchor' occurs 'We have fled for refuge,' declares the writer to the Hebrews, 'to lay hold upon the hope set before us: which hope we have as an anchor of the soul, sure and steadfast.' There it is then. Anchor number one: *Hope*.

Is that part of your ship's equipment? As long as a man has hope in his heart, life cannot destroy him. It may hurt him, but it will not break him. As long as hope holds out, he will weather the roughest storm. It is when hope goes — it is when things are going wrong, and the heart grows heavy as lead, and buoyancy gives way to cynicism, and life looks futile and contemptible — it is then the ship goes under.

Our anchor — Hope! Only, mark you, it must be *Christian* hope — not just a vague temperamental optimism, not a continual pathetic waiting for 'something to turn up', like Mr. Micawber in the story, not a mere indulging in sentimental day-dreams or building castles in the air. That is no anchor for the soul's time of need. That snaps at the first real strain. It is Christian hope we are needing. And what is Christian hope? It is the attitude towards life of a man who has gazed upon the face of God the Father.

St. Paul once said this fine thing: 'Now the God of hope fill you with joy and peace, that ye may abound in hope, through the power of the Holy Ghost.' *The God of hope* — that is, the God who creates hope, the God whose revealed character is the basis of all hope. That is the anchor.

There was a psalmist once, whose barque was tempest-tossed and foundering, groaning in every timber, and heading straight for where the white spray was dashing on the deadly rocks — when, suddenly, he bethought him of his anchor! 'Why art thou cast down, O my soul? Why art thou disquieted within me? Hope thou in God!' And that anchor, let down upon the everlasting rock, held and saved him. The God of hope! The God who brings a hope as bright as the radiance in the eyes of Jesus. The God you can count on though plans be ruined, and dreams go out, and the things you have longed for most of all never come to you in this life, and your heart feels like to break.

There is a story which Principal Rainy used to tell about a man in Edinburgh, who was a bad character and a confirmed law-breaker, often in the hands of the police. He had only one redeeming feature in his life — his love for his little girl, who was an only child, the very image of her dead mother.

He committed burglary, and was put into prison. During the term of his sentence, his child died. On the day when he came out, he learned of her death. It was a shattering blow. He could not go back to the house. He was simply broken. In his wild and bitter distraction, he resolved that when night came he would fling himself over the Dean Bridge, and end it all. At midnight he stood on the bridge. He was climbing the parapet, when suddenly, for no reason that he could think of (as he himself said afterwards) there flashed into his mind the opening words of the creed — 'I believe in God the Father Almighty.' And he stepped back. Again it came, clearer and stronger this time — 'God the Father Almighty!' He knew nothing of God, but he did know something of fatherhood. 'Why,' he found himself saying, 'if that is what God is, if God is like that, then I can trust Him with my lassie — and with myself!' And from that moment death receded: life began anew. At the last gasp, the anchor Hope had held!

> 'But yet the Lord, that is on high,
>   is more of might by far
> Than noise of many waters is,
>   or great sea-billows are.'

'Which hope we have as an anchor of the soul.' Can you say it? Have you the anchor on board? You will win the haven yet!

'They cast four anchors out, and wished for the day'. Hope is one. But one is not adequate for safety. We must find another. I want to bring before you now what I believe to be one of the best and most blessed of all the anchors of the soul, especially in the stormy seas of youth. Its name is *Duty*. That is our anchor number two.

But let us be honest about this. Are there not times when

we rebel against duty? We kick against what we think to be
the drudgery that cribs and cabins and confines us. We sometimes almost curse the fate that nails us to our daily discipline. Why should we be shackled? Why should we be held
down? Why should our life not be our own? Why is there
not more freedom to do as we like? Why should we have to
keep at it, day in, day out, until somewhere down the years
death comes and ends the tale? The whole system, cries the
rebel soul, is hard and cruel and unjust.

Believe me, it is only blindness that thinks that. And if
you should sit down one day, with a pen and a sheet of paper,
to write down, before God and your own soul, the things
which have blessed you most since you came into this world
right up to this present moment, I would advise you to put
duty high up on the list — not indeed first (for the grace of
God must stand there), but bracketed next with human love.
Why? Because it is the sheet-anchor of your soul! And I
pray you to remember this, that there are ships sailing the
seas of life today, souls of men and women young and old,
that would have been smashed and wrecked and done for
scores of times, if they had not had that anchor to steady
them and hold them safe.

Take an illustration. Take Josephine Butler, the great
nineteenth-century heroine and benefactress of broken and
outcast womanhood. Everyone knows how that noble
career began. She had returned home one day from a journey
and Evangeline, her only daughter — who was the light of
her life — was watching for her coming. When the carriage
reached the door, the child in her eagerness ran from the
window, leaned over the balustrade, and fell — and lay
dying at her mother's feet. Terrible beyond words was the
darkness of that day's grief; but at last Mrs. Butler turned
for help and comfort to the home of an old, saintly Quaker
woman who lived nearby. And this was the message she
received. 'God hath taken to Himself her whom thou didst

love; but there are many forlorn young hearts who need that mother-love of thine. Go to — Street, No. —, and knock.' She went. It turned out to be a refuge where forty young lives, once lost and in peril, were being cared for with all the kindness of true Christian sympathy and understanding. Into that labour of love Mrs. Butler threw herself; and so found herself committed to the high task that was to make her one of the greatest social reformers of the century. Thus in the day of her bitterest need, when she thought she had reached the end of everything, the end of faith, the end of love, the end of God — it was the call of duty that steadied her, and calmed her, and gave her the mastery of her soul.

Thank God for duty — that mighty anchor! Thank God for the providence which decreed that only in the sweat of his brow should man eat bread. Thank God for the tasks that give you something better to do than brooding and introspection. Thank God for the sheer hard toil that keeps the seven devils from getting into the swept and garnished house. Thank God for the things that must be done, even though the heavens should crash and fall. Thank God for duty! It will hold the ship until the day break and the shadows flee away.

Our first anchor is Hope, our second Duty. Is that enough? 'They cast four anchors out, and wished for the day', and hope and duty still need reinforcing. Our anchor number three is *Prayer*.

God help the ship that leaves the harbour without that anchor on board! But so many of them do. And so many who once possessed it have long since cast it away.

It is extraordinary that there are people today genuinely trying to be Christians, and yet never praying from one week's end to another. How can the spiritual life be vital under such conditions? How can God be real? How can religion seem anything more than a dim, vague idealism that does not really count?

I do want to make this clear. The man who does not pray, who does not have even five minutes a day in his own room face to face with God and heart to heart with Christ, is simply playing with his soul. And if he is the father of a family, he may be playing with his children's souls. I want to ask him: What does he believe? He says he believes in God the Father Almighty. But does he? He says he believes there is such a thing as the soul. Does he? He says he believes we are moving on to eternity. Does he? Has he ever sat down and thought out what a single one of these great beliefs involves, for himself, if it is really true? Would not half an hour's hard, honest thinking about it drive him to his knees?

I am not saying that prayer is everything. I am not saying that without prayer a man cannot make a decent show in life at all. But I am saying that without prayer there is no Christian life possible that is worthy of the name. Why? Because it is down the channel of prayer that the power of God gets into a man. And you cannot live the life for which Jesus stands, you cannot love your neighbour as you ought, you cannot keep the spiritual outlook upon the world— without the power of God to help you to do it.

And what about temptation? Let me put this to the young men and women here. Do you know the difference between meeting some particular temptation on a day when you have prayed your morning prayers and looked into the steady eyes of Christ, and meeting that same temptation on another day when you have no such backing and reinforcement? Servants of the King of kings, you who would fain drive a straight path for yourselves through the dangers and difficulties of this tangled and perplexing age, will you remember that everything depends — your discipleship, your future, your peace of mind, your soul's true health — everything depends upon whether you yourselves are men and women of prayer? God has given you the anchor. Use it!

Am I speaking to someone here who, for one reason or

another, has lost the prayer habit? Someone who would feel desperately awkward and self-conscious about starting it again tonight? Friend, do not get angry with me. Do not tell me it is none of my business. If God wants me to talk to you at all, He wants me to talk to you about this. We are not here in this Church for amusement. We are not here to spend a comfortable hour, and rise up and go away just the same as we came. We are here to meet God. And no man can meet God and be just the same. This matter of prayer is vital and decisive, as vital as anything in your life at this moment. And if you go to rest tonight unpraying, this word that I am speaking now is going to haunt you — for your own heart tells you it is true. And just think — it would be so easy to start again tonight; so worth while to conquer that feeling of strangeness and self-consciousness — for the sake of God and your own soul! A day may come, a day of storm and stress, when you will be driven to cry to Him, scourged into it by life itself. Oh, get back your daily prayers — lest, when that hour come, you find your anchor gone!

Hope, Duty, Prayer — three strong, staunch anchors of the soul. But once again the question arises, Is that sufficient? 'They cast four anchors out.' One more we need. You know its name. It is the greatest of them all. It is *the Cross of Christ*.

Do you know what it means to feel the grip of that cross upon your soul?

> 'O dearly, dearly has He loved,
>   And we must love Him too.'

I wonder if there is any anchor in this world like love. When the storms are on the deep, is there any safety like the power of a great affection?

The whole of life bears witness to the fact that it is the personal element that saves. Advice, ethical codes, the religion that deals in '-ologies', and 'isms' — all that may simply leave a man cold and untouched. But if he loves — if he loves — thrice-armed is he against the foe!

A young life goes out into this dangerous world, where countless unknown temptations lurk. What is going to hold him straight and true? Not any moral philosophy, not any copy-book maxims, not any wise, well-meaning advice. No. But the love of the home and the parents who have sacrificed for him. The anchor! See him when temptation comes. Hear his soul's brave answer to the tempter — 'How can I do this thing, and sin against love?' It is these personal relationships that are life's master-forces.

And that is why God, two thousand years ago, personalised religion. 'The Word' — the abstract thing, the -ism, the -ology — 'was made Flesh' — the personal element, Jesus; that so religion as the keeping of a law might be finished, and in its place might come religion as a personal passion for Christ. And when the cross of God's uttermost on Calvary has got its grip upon a man, when he has felt the strength of the love that will not let him go — what an anchor of the soul is there, stronger than the waves of life, and mightier than the whirlwind of death!

I am going to finish with this. You have read Tennyson's tale of King Arthur's knights and the Round Table; and you remember that loveliest of characters, Sir Galahad, who with his own eyes was to see the Holy Grail, because of the great purity of his heart. Recall his words:

> 'And hither am I come; and never yet
> Hath what thy sister taught me first to see,
> This Holy Thing, fail'd from my side, nor come
> Cover'd, but moving with me night and day,
> Fainter by day, but always in the night

Blood-red, and sliding down the blacken'd marsh
Blood-red, and on the naked mountain top
Blood-red, and in the sleeping mere below
Blood-red. And in the strength of this I rode,
Shattering all evil customs everywhere,
And broke thro' all, and in the strength of this
Come victor.'

Listen, young knight of Jesus Christ! You have seen the cross — blood-red on the hill of Calvary, blood-red with 'love divine, all loves excelling,' blood-red for your redemption, blood-red with God's great agony. The cross — its very shape is like an anchor — binds, holds, grips your soul with grace and mercy. In the love of this, be pure. In the grip of this, stand steady. In the strength of this, come victor. The cross — your anchor — for ever and for ever!

XII

God and the Moral Struggle

'Now Elisha was fallen sick of his sickness whereof he died. And Joash the king of Israel came down unto him, and wept over his face, and said, O my father, my father, the chariot of Israel, and the horsemen thereof. And Elisha said unto him, Take bow and arrows. And he took unto him bow and arrows. And he said to the king of Israel, Put thine hand upon the bow.' — 2 KINGS xiii. 14–16.

LET US TRY TO SEE THIS YOUNG MAN, THIS JOASH, KING OF Israel, to see him both in his strength and in his weakness; and may God help us to take the lesson that is here, and apply it to ourselves today.

The scene is set at a death-bed. It is the death-bed of a man of God. The long, turbulent life of Elisha is almost over. The voice that had so often startled the world, crying 'Thus saith the Lord', is only a whisper now, trailing off into the last eternal silence. It is a poor, unpretentious room where he lies — a humble lodging on the city's eastern wall. But there at the bedside stands the king. And the young king's heart is desolate as he thinks of the void which Elisha's passing is going to leave. 'O my father,' he cries, for he feels almost like a son towards this dying man of God, and this is a cry of orphanhood, 'O my father, my father, the chariot of Israel, and the horsemen thereof!'

Was that not a glorious tribute to the influence of consecrated character? For what the king meant was — 'You, my father, have been a greater strength to the nation than all its armies and navies. You, by your life and character and vision of God, have been our true salvation. You, alone by yourself, just by being yourself, have been chariots and horsemen to Israel!' What a tribute to the sheer power of goodness!

And here is the clear message it brings to us today: it is character alone that is a nation's wealth—not armaments, not gold reserves, not political prestige, but God-filled men. You sometimes hear people speaking disparagingly — it was Nietzsche who set the fashion — of what they call 'mere goodness', as though for any practical purpose, for achieving results in this problematical and often heartbreaking world, the things for which religion stands just did not count at all. But, thank God, there is a growing consensus of conviction now that that is the stupidest of mistakes, and that the one hope of this nation and of every nation and of the whole world is not chariots and horsemen, but lives with God's stamp upon them, and Christ's character burnt into them! Such lives are the chariots and the horsemen.

And that is why ordinary statistics can mislead so wildly. One God-filled personality may throw out all our usual calculations. Ten righteous men, said God, would have saved Sodom, when whole battalions of unbelievers could not have done it. And you remember Gideon's strange stroke of generalship: he dismissed his original thirty-two thousand and started all over again with a paltry three hundred. Paltry? No. For everyone of them was God's man!

It is told that once during the American Civil War, a detachment of Sheridan's men, caught in a tight corner, broke and fled and galloped away for their lives: and just then Sheridan himself came riding up. Taking in the situation at a glance, he rose in his stirrups, waved his sword above his head, and shouted, 'Men, we are going the other way!' Whereupon the fleeing host stopped dead, and for a moment there was not a sound; but then with a great cry they turned, wheeled in their tracks, and smashed their way back to victory. One man's influence! 'My father, my father,' cried Joash, 'you have been worth chariots and horsemen to Israel!' Mere goodness, shall we still say slightingly? Mere religion? It was the Wesleyan revival, declares Lecky the historian, which saved England in the eighteenth century from the horrors of a French Revolution. And it is men and women revived in the Spirit of the living God who are the one real hope of this uneasy and distracted world, which stands listening to the storm-winds muttering in the distance, and to the earthquake rumblings beneath its feet. This is the plain unvarnished truth, God's writing on the wall. Wanted — men of character, men like Christ! The chariot of Israel and the horsemen thereof!

But now let us move on to what is more personal in the story. Here is this young king looking disconsolately into a desolate future in which he will have to stand alone, with no Elisha to lean upon. But suddenly his sad reverie is interrupted. The dying man on the bed stirs, and something of the old light is kindled again within his eyes. 'Take bow and arrows,' he commands. And Joash, wondering, takes them. 'Now come near, and let me lay my hands on yours'; and the prophet lays his wasted, trembling hands on the steady hands of the young king, as though to put something of God's Spirit and power into them (I wonder if Christ's pierced hands have ever gripped ours like that?) — and then, 'Open that window to the east,' says Elisha. And the young man flings it wide. 'Now shoot!' And Joash draws back the arrow on the bow, and lets it fly; and as it flashes on its way, the dying voice cries aloud, 'The arrow of the Lord's deliverance — the arrow of the Lord!'

Of course, it was all symbolical. For the way to issue a challenge to your enemy in those days was to stand on the verge of his land and shoot an arrow into the territory you meant to conquer. And Joash recognised at once what the symbol implied. It was as though the dying man had said:

'Remember, when I am gone, you are not to bow down to Syria nor acquiesce in its tyranny! You are to challenge it in the name of the Lord God of hosts. You are to stand up to this evil thing, and defy it!' The arrow of the Lord's deliverance!

Is that not a message that we need to hear? Cross out Syria, and put in our own stubborn temptations — do we not need to hear it? What a mass of unheroic spiritual acquiescence our lives can show! We are so apt to accept ourselves as we are, and to be content with that. Perhaps we even say, 'Oh, I am not cut out to be a saint or anything of that kind. I am quite satisfied if I can lead a decent average life; and as for those recurring temptations — to be slack about my prayers, for instance, or to be quick to take offence or to leave thought unguarded and out of control — do such things really matter so very much after all?' And so we just knuckle down to Syria! 'But they do matter,' says the Word of God here to us quite bluntly, 'they do! And it is not brave in the least, it is not manly, it is not honest, to live as though they did not. Out with your challenge! Shoot your arrow. Claim that uncaptured territory for Christ!'

Tolstoy, in a dramatic passage, has described a man sitting in a boat which has been pushed off from an unknown shore; and he has been shown the opposite shore, and given a pair of oars, and left alone. Straight out into the stream he rows; but then the current gets hold of him and deflects him. Other boats are there; some have thrown their oars away, a few are struggling against the stream, most are gliding with it quite content. 'Is this the way?' he asks some of them; and a chorus of voices replies, 'Of course it is! What did you think? There can be no other way.' And so he drifts on; but suddenly he grows conscious of a sound, menacing, terrible — the roar of rapids: and the man comes to himself remembers what he had forgotten — the oars, the course, the opposite shore — and madly he begins to row upstream against the current, crying 'Fool that I was to drift!' He rows on, until safety is reached. Now, says Tolstoy, that current is the tradition of the world, the oars are freewill, the opposite shore is God!

But how many are content to drift with the stream! 'Good-bye to our daydreams', wrote Captain Scott pathetically when he found himself forestalled at the Pole; and many a young life that once dreamed great dreams of character and God has come to that today — 'Good-bye to our daydreams'. Some of you will remember the terribly poignant passage in Dickens's story, where Sidney Carton — 'the man of good abilities and good emotions, incapable of their directed exercise, incapable of his own help and his own happiness, sensible of the blight on him, and resigning himself to let it eat him away' — was walking through the lifeless desert of London's streets in the grey twilight of the dawn. Suddenly he paused, for there in front of him was a vision — the vision of a life, his very life, crowned with nobleness and self-denying perseverance and usefulness and love. But the vision was only a mocking mirage: a moment, and it was gone. He climbed to his lonely garret, and flung himself down in his clothes on his neglected bed, and his pillow was wet with wasted tears. There you have a man acquiescing in his own temptations, taking them for granted, too tame to stand up and strike a blow for freedom. This is all that I have it in my power to be, he says, and for the rest — why worry?

We often feel like that; but sometimes, thank God, we see that acquiescing spirit as it is — a dismal, craven following of the line of least resistance. 'O God,' cried Kagawa of Japan, on the day when the new life first stirred within his breast, 'I want to be like Christ! O God, make me like Christ!' The most important transaction in life, said Carlyle, describing his own experience, was on a day when — after years of acquiescence, years of being dragged at the chariot-wheels of his own tyrant fear, with its taunting voice ever ringing in his ears, 'Thou art mine, my bond-slave, mine' — suddenly something within him sprang up and took control, and looked that tyrant in the face. 'I am not thine,' it cried, 'but my own, and free! And I hate, hate, despise thee!' That is the spirit. 'I promise before God in heaven,' cried Abraham Lincoln in his youth, watching the tragedy of a slave-market, 'if ever I get a chance to hit this thing, I will hit it hard!' You have a chance to hit that tyrant thing in you — now. Don't say you have to lie down to it. Don't say that there it is, and there it will always be. Don't say it does not matter. Hit it hard — smite it with the lightnings of God!

'Grant us the will to fashion as we feel,
  Grant us the strength to labour as we know,
  Grant us the purpose, ribbed and edged with steel,
    To strike the blow.'

That is what these weak hearts of ours are needing, a purpose ribbed and edged with steel — and Christ alone can create it. Lord Jesus, make us strong!

But that is not all. One bold stroke at Syria, as Elisha saw, was not enough. See what happened next. 'Take the bow again,' said the dying prophet to the young king, 'and take this time a whole quiver of arrows.' And Joash obeyed. 'Now smite upon the ground,' said Elisha. And the king shot three times upon the ground, and laid the bow down. Whereupon, 'Alas!' cried the prophet. 'Why did you stop? You should have smitten many times, for then you would have utterly conquered Syria — whereas now you will smite it only thrice!'

Now again, of course, there was a parable behind it. And the meaning, the spiritual message for ourselves, shines clearly through. 'Remember,' it says to us, 'you who are battling with temptation — remember it is a stubborn foe you are facing. A good beginning is not enough, one bold defiance is never adequate. You have to keep it up. You have to fight on, and hope on, and pray on — until the thing is dead!'

Here, let us say, is a young man who joined the Church by profession of faith. And on the night of his dedication, he looked into the eyes of Christ and promised to be faithful until death. From that hour, everything was to be new. He would break once and for all with the inward tempter. He would go out and put some wrong personal relationship right. He would make a fresh start with his prayers. He would tear the dearest idol from the throne that should be Christ's. And he did. And there was joy among the angels in heaven. But that was — when? Last year, shall we say? It seems an unreal, far-off story now. Perhaps he is even secretly ashamed of it. So much can happen in a year! Somehow the high mood passed. The vision faded. The flame died upon the altar. Back crept the beloved temptation. Home came the dethroned idol. Gradually, imperceptibly, Christ's standards were toned down. Steadily the world's pressure worked its will. Others did things, and thought nothing about them — why should not he? Was he to miss so much? It was folly to aim too high. The easier and more comfortable road must do. A year ago? Surely a lifetime ago — that night of dedication, that eager vow to Jesus Christ! Oh, surely not last year? Yes, just last year. And today?

> 'Whither is fled the visionary gleam?
> Where is it now, the glory and the dream?'

Almost everyone has phases of religious feeling, and it is easy in those high moments to stand up and smite the foe in the name of God; but to keep campaigning till the foe is broken, finished, dead — that is where we fail. 'I'm all fits', wrote Haydon the artist to a friend, 'fits of work, fits of idleness, fits of reading, fits of religion.' And in the moral struggle, that leads nowhere.

Good Mr. Pliable, in Bunyan's story, made a splendid

start. 'This is the life, this is the life,' he kept telling himself, when he had fallen in on the march to the Celestial City; and he kept plucking at Christian's sleeve. 'Faster, man, faster!' he cried impatiently, 'Why are you dawdling? Come on, let us mend our pace — let us run!' And then the Slough of Despond engulfed them; and while Christian set his teeth, and struggled valiantly through to the other side, Pliable, with all his bubbling eagerness suddenly evaporated, was crying, 'Help me out! Help me out! If I escape with my life, you can possess the brave country alone, for me — I am going home.' And next moment he was running back down the road by which he had come, a poor bedraggled thing with mud in his clothes, and mud in his hair, and mud in his very soul: and that was how his bid for freedom ended. And how it has ended thousands of times!

Thinking of which, this old Book declares with disconcerting directness — 'Ye have not yet resisted unto blood, striving against sin', and lays its finger on that as the real clue to our spiritual commonplaceness. And if we answer back, 'But I *have* resisted, I really did try to conquer this temptation, I did fight the thing, and it is simply no use', if we make that our defence, 'Yes, yes', it continues, 'you resisted — in a way: but look at your soul — *where are the blood-marks*? None? None? And yet you talk about "resisting"? Friend, climb Calvary! See what resistance meant to Jesus! See the blood — from His head, His hands, his feet, His side, His heart — sorrow and love flowing mingled down! And is it to mean not one drop of blood for you? You are not in earnest.'

There was a great moment once in the Roman Senate, when Rome had been humbled on the battlefield by the might of Carthage, and pessimistic voices were counselling surrender. 'It is the only thing to do,' they said, 'we have fought and we have been beaten: now let us make some compromise.' 'Stop!' cried an old senator, leaping to his

feet. 'Remember this — Rome does not go to battle: Rome
goes to war!' Remember this, in the fight with your temptations — Christ's men do not go to battle, they go to war!
They refuse to quit the field till the foe is vanquished.

You are to conquer on the scene of old defeats. Simon
Peter, I feel sure, would gladly have shunned Jerusalem,
connected as it was with the most shameful memory of his
life, a memory of desertion, denial, and defeat. Yet the first
command he received from the risen Christ was, 'Begin at
Jerusalem! Go and preach My gospel there. Unfurl the flag
again on the very spot where you hauled it down!' And I
think Peter cried, 'No, Christ, no! Not there — anywhere
but there. North, south, east, or west I'll go — but not
there!' 'I say you must!' commanded Christ; 'Go, turn
defeat to victory!' And he did. And so must we. Don't be a
Joash, striking once or twice and then desisting: be like all
the saints who have cried — 'Rejoice not against me, O mine
enemy; when I fall, I shall arise!'

And Christ goes with you in this. That is the meaning of
'grace'. One might preach self-reliance and self-effort to the
day of doom, and only drive men deeper to despair. But
to throw yourself in your weakness upon God, to know the
reinforcement of a Saviour at your side, to open the inmost
recesses of your being to the power of the Holy Spirit — that
is the Christian way. That is hope reborn, and courage renewed. That is the dawn of victory.

Give Christ a spirit like that, and the tide of battle will
turn. For — this is the last thing I want to say to you today,
and it is enormously cheering to know it — it is possible, by
prayer and persistence and the grace of God in Christ,
possible even in this present life, mark you, to gain victories
over temptation that are final and complete, final in the
sense that that particular temptation will never trouble you
again. This is no optimistic fancy: it is proved experience.
Sisyphus, in the old story, had a dreadful fate: always he

had to keep pushing the great mass of rock up the slopes of the hill, and always when he was nearing the summit, when he was thinking — 'This time I shall do it, I am almost there — steady now, steady! — one touch more and it is done' — always it came rolling down, tumbling and dashing to the foot; and he had to begin again, and so on to all eternity. But God means no child of His to be a moral Sisyphus! 'Our soul,' cried an excited psalmist long ago, 'is escaped as a bird out of the snare of the fowlers: the snare is broken, and we are escaped!' And sometimes, when you have battled long and hard and prayerfully with an evil thing, there comes a day when you suddenly realise that the pull of it, the lure and magnetism and fascination of it, are not there any longer: the snare is broken, the bird escaped — your soul flies free! What a tremendous thrill there is in the words of Exodus, spoken to a people who for long weary years had felt the scourge of Egypt on their souls: 'The Egyptians whom ye have seen today, ye shall see them again no more for ever.' All those bitter, humiliating years, and then — no more again for ever! It does happen, even here in this present life.

Once there were three crosses on an eastern hill, and round them there was thick darkness and silence, darkness as of midnight, silence as of death; when suddenly, stabbing the darkness, shattering the silence, came from the centre cross a cry, a shout — 'It is finished!' Take courage. This is the glory of the fight of faith, that one day God, looking out from heaven, may hear His own Son's words upon your lips, that one day out of the darkness and silence of your struggle there may come the cry — 'It is finished! Finished the temptation! Finished the lure of it! Finished the power of it! Finished the tyranny of it! Other foes there may be yet to meet, but this one — never again. This snare is broken. This Egyptian is dead on the seashore. Glory be to Christ — it is finished!'

XIII

The Magnetism of the Unseen

'Whom having not seen, ye love; in whom, though now ye see Him not, yet believing, ye rejoice with joy unspeakable and full of glory: receiving the end of your faith, even the salvation of your souls.' — 1 PETER i. 8, 9.

I FANCY THAT MANY A CHRISTIAN, ENCOUNTERING THESE words of Peter's — 'Whom having not seen' — would answer at once, 'But I *have* seen Him! You can't shake my certainty of that. It is the very foundation of my personal religion, that Christ and I have met.' I think many of us would say that. And quite rightly. For if the unspoken demand that the Christian preacher hears from a congregation gathering in the Church for worship, is 'Sir, we would see Jesus'; if he realises that he has been ordained to his ministry, not to waste his time and theirs on genial generalties, but to do something to meet that demand for the vision of the Son of God — then it must be possible to see Christ still. I will go further, and say that unless all the saints have been mistaken; unless the hymn we so often sing at Holy Communion — 'Here, O my Lord, I see Thee face to face' — is just a form of words, and nothing more; unless you are prepared to deny the witness of your own heart which, looking back across the years, can single out one place after another and say, 'There and there God came to me in Jesus'; unless you are going to write down the inmost convictions of ten thousand souls as the mere vapourings of overheated imagination — the fact stands beyond challenge that men can see Christ today. Take a congregation like this. If only it were possible to have a record of all the personal encounters with Christ represented by such a congregation — encounters in private prayer and at secret crossroads of decision, encounters in young manhood and young womanhood and in the gloaming of life's evening, encounters in quiet moods, and in sudden moments of desperate stress and need — if all that could be recorded, what a marvellous and moving story it would be! Men do see Jesus still. It does happen.

> 'And earth hath ne'er so dear a spot
>   As where I meet with Thee.'

And yet — 'Whom having not seen', says Peter. For, after all, none of us has seen Christ just as Peter saw Him. To Peter, as to the other disciples, Jesus had been a physical presence. He had eaten and drunk with them, and trudged the dusty roads of Galilee with them, and slept with them at nights beneath the open sky. Do you not envy them that intimacy? I am sure the thought sometimes comes to us — 'If only I had seen Jesus like that, how different everything would have been! If I could have lived with Him as they did, could have consulted Him about the personal difficulties that make a tangle of my life, how much simpler life would have been! One single day with Jesus would have solved all my private problems, and straightened out my soul's confusions, and made me a new being altogether.' Has that thought never crossed your mind?

> 'Dim tracts of time divide
> Those golden days from me;
> Thy voice comes strange o'er years of change;
>   How can we follow Thee?
>
> Comes faint and far Thy voice
> From vales of Galilee;

Thy vision fades in ancient shades;
How should we follow Thee?'

But natural as such thoughts may be, they are really quite mistaken. One fact they are ignoring, the fact Paul fixed on when he said 'Christ, being raised from the dead, dieth no more'; which means that what Calvary and the Resurrection did was to set the Spirit of Jesus loose in the world, untrammelled and alive for ever, freer actually than He ever was in the days of Galilee, and nearer now to His own than when they roamed together through the cornfields and the vineyards, or kept vigil beneath the Syrian stars.

It is no myth nor make-believe when men declare that they have had intimate dealings with Jesus, and have found His friendship the most vivid reality of life. 'Whom having not seen, ye love'.

And so we turn to the main burden of the apostle's message. What he is trying to do here is something rather daring: it is nothing less than to define the central Christian experience in a single sentence; and you will observe that he has packed it all into four words, four short, decisive verbs. 'Ye love — ye believe — ye rejoice — ye receive.' That, he declares, is what it means to be a Christian. That, throughout the ages, has been the high road of salvation.

Let us examine this fourfold progression. First stands the verb '*Ye love*'. Now that immediately suggests the question — What, in its essence, *is* the Christian religion?

Not a philosophy of life. Certainly it will give you a philosophy, for the faith of Jesus is ultimately the only thing that can make sense of the universe. But that is not what its essence is. You need more than a philosophy to hold you steady when the storms begin to blow, or when your dreams are lying wrecked, or when the demons of temptation have leapt upon your soul.

Not a moral code. Certainly it will provide you with that — the most sublime and noble ethic in the world. But that is not its essence. Men are not set on fire for God by anything so intolerably distant and impersonal as moral maxims and ethical idealisms.

Not a social creed. Certainly it will give you that: Christ has been behind more social reforms than any other leader who has ever appeared upon the earth. But that is not its essence. No amount of merely social passion can change lives or work the miracle of regeneration; and you cannot build the Kingdom of heaven out of men and women not redeemed.

The essence of Christ's religion is none of these things. It is a personal attachment. It is a response in love to the most fascinating Personality who ever walked this earth. Theologies may sometimes raise more perplexities than they solve, and manuals of ethics may seem dull and strangely out of touch with life; but if you should one day be confronted with the ancient question which confronted Simon Peter, 'Do you love Christ?' I know what your answer, in simple utter sincerity, would be. 'Love Jesus? Why, I'd die for Him!' Well, that is religion — not a vague abstraction, but a wonderful affection; not a tiresome argument, but a tremendous friendship; not an intricate and uninspired philosophy, but an inspired and thrilling love; not a drudging at the grindstone of a dingy routine morality, but 'Christ in you the hope of glory'.

> 'How can I choose but love Thee, God's dear Son,
> O Jesus, loveliest and most loving One?
> Were there no heaven to gain, no hell to flee,
> For what Thou art alone I must love Thee.'

'Whom having not seen, ye love.'

Then the apostle proceeds: 'In whom though now ye see Him not, yet believing.' There is his second verb. Ye love, and — *ye believe*. Now it is this that keeps the love in Christianity from growing sentimental. For what is belief in Christ? What, for that matter, is belief in anyone? It is *love going into action*. It is love proving itself in life. It is love staking its soul upon the worth of the one beloved. Kagawa of Japan was trying to explain what Christianity meant to him. 'I am God's gambler,' he cried. 'For Him I have wagered my last mite.' That is belief — not intellectual assent to a theory, but the throwing in of a life. In the stirring words of Martin Luther, 'The only faith which makes a Christian is that which casts itself on God for life or death.'

It is easy to see, as I have suggested, that, apart from this, love might degenerate into sentimentalism. There is a type of religion which sings, with suitable emotion, the love songs of the Church, without ever so much as giving a thought to what an old saint once called 'the stormy north side of Jesus Christ'.

> 'Take my love; my Lord, I pour
> At Thy feet its treasure-store' —

and all the time, the man is clinging to something which he knows ought to have been cast out long ago, or he is refusing to forgive some injury, or he is easily offended, or he is self-approving and consequential, or he is slack about his prayers.

> 'Take myself, and I will be
> Ever, only, all for Thee' —

and all the time, there is something in his life towards which, in the stern, downright words of the Book of Revelation,

Christ's eyes are as a flame of fire! To talk of loving Christ on that basis is purely artificial. To worship Christ, without bringing life into line with such worship, is definitely more dangerous for a man's own soul than if he never worshipped at all. But the mark of Christian faith, says Peter, is not that it uses glowing love-language about Jesus: it is that it surrenders its life to the object of its love. Faith means being permeated with Christ's spirit. It means being captured by Christ's character. It means, as it meant to Christ, that you risk doing the will of God, even when there is a cross in it. Nothing sentimental about that love! It is strong with the strength of the eternal hills, and beautiful with the terrible beauty that once flamed up to God on Calvary. 'Whom having not seen, ye love; in whom, though now ye see Him not, ye believe.'

Follow the apostle's progress further. Ye love, ye believe, '*ye rejoice* with joy unspeakable and full of glory'. Do you trace the connection? You love Jesus — that is first; and that love leads on to an offering of your life to Jesus — to belief and faith and irrevocable surrender; and that offering of life in turn produces a new kind of thrill never known before. For here is the great discovery you make; there is no joy on earth like the joy of being committed.

It is the swithering and undecided attitude that is dull and dreary and never sings. You cannot be happy — it is a psychological and spiritual impossibility — as long as you are refusing the daring of your own soul.

Why is the New Testament the most joyous book in the world? It is because these men and women were committed up to the very hilt. They had crossed their Rubicon, and were far too deeply involved with Christ on His great adventure ever to extricate themselves or to draw back. 'All things are ours,' they cried, 'for we are Christ's, and Christ is God's'; and sang their Halelujah Choruses across the world, and went singing down to the ghastly shambles of the Roman arena, and marched singing to the throne of God.

And if we could show the world today that being committed to Christ is no tame, humdrum, sheltered monotony, but the most fascinating and exciting adventure the human spirit can ever know — 'joy unspeakable and full of glory' — then thousands of strong and stalwart lives that have been holding back from Christ and looking askance at the Church and standing outside the Kingdom would come crowding in to His allegiance; and there might be such a revival as the world has not witnessed since Pentecost.

This is no empty dream. There are signs now that the age is ripe for a great return to Christ. What are we witnessing throughout Europe and the world today? We are witnessing a demand for two things — a leader, and a cause. A living leader — not any longer a political theory or a revolutionary idea, but the theory incarnate in a man, the idea crystallised in a person, the word made flesh — that is what men are wanting: hence the hero-worship offered today to a Stalin, a Gandhi, a Hitler. And along with that, men demand a cause, something which will lay the most absolute claims upon them, something to which they can commit themselves sacrificially, body, mind, and soul. Nationalism and Communism may be at each other's throats, and their conflict productive of chaos in the world; but at least they are alike in this — and mark you, it is the central thing about them, the point at which they are wiser in their generation than the children of light, certainly wiser than a reduced, misguided, milk-and-water Christianity that thinks to attract men by not asking too much — alike in this, that each claims unhesitatingly a man's all, everything he has to give. That is what the spirit of the age is clamouring for — the leader who will really lead, the cause that will challenge to sacrifice. And therefore, is not this the day of Christ's opportunity? A leader? Here is the only leader whose name is not doomed to be writ in water, a leader with a magnetism surely irresistible. A cause? Here is a cause that demands every ounce of valour and devotion a man can bring to it, a cause that does not shrink to speak of sacrifice, a cause that may burn a man out in its service — for God is a consuming fire. It is high time we realised that it is no use setting a mild and undemanding half-Christianity against a militant, masterful paganism; no use setting some poor apologetic replica of Christ against the deified heroes of the age. But to see the real Christ, 'strong Son of God, immortal Love,' to stand committed to the real Christian adventure, the serving of Jesus the King with every breath of your body and every beat of your heart — that is a thrill such as no other leader or cause on this earth can ever generate. That is the answer to the heart's demand for a passion and a high crusade. That is the joy unspeakable and full of glory.

And now we take the last step with the apostle. Ye love, ye believe, ye rejoice, '*ye receive* the salvation of your souls.' The word 'salvation' is like the cross that purchased it: it reaches up to heaven, and goes down to hell, and its arms embrace the world. For the past, it brings forgiveness; for the present, the power of the Spirit; and for the future, life for evermore.

And, says Peter, ye receive it. You do not win it, for no man can do that. You do not earn it, for it is not a wage. You do not buy it, for it is not for sale. You receive it. You bow your head, with pride all broken down, and take the gift from Jesus' hand.

Well, will you? Some of us are hovering on the verge of the Kingdom still, outside the authentic, redeeming experience, not because the next step is too difficult, but because it is so simple. 'Ask, and ye shall receive.' 'If ye know how to give good gifts unto your children, how much more shall your heavenly Father give the Holy Spirit to them that ask Him?'

But have you asked? Have you ever come to the point of saying — 'Lord, the struggle is too hard for me. But Thou hast said Thou wouldst take charge of my life, if I would turn it over to Thee. Lord, I do hand it over now. Take charge, as Thou hast promised?' Have you ever risen from your knees, after a prayer like that, believing that the gift had come, and gone out to face life in the reinforcement of that belief? So it is that men receive God's crowning gift, the salvation of their souls.

And if you have never quite taken God at His word about this, feeling perhaps that the offered remedy for your problem was too simple to be true, will you not thrust that deadening doubt aside, and make one real trial of a promise for which on Calvary Christ pledged His honour, and take God at His word today?

XIV

Holy Alliances

'What therefore God hath joined together, let not man put asunder.' — MARK x. 9.

LET US TAKE THIS DEEP SAYING OF OUR LORD OUT OF ITS original setting. As it stands here, it was spoken in answer to one particular question, the question of the Pharisees about marriage and divorce; but like so many of the Master's sayings, its application goes far beyond the original intention. The circumstances which first elicited this profound remark of Jesus by no means exhaust its significance. Indeed, what we have here is not simply a ruling on one isolated problem: it is a principle which can be seen running through the whole structure of life. 'What God hath joined together, let not man put asunder.' A moment's pondering will reveal to you the unsuspected width and range of that remark; and what I wish to do now is to suggest some of these God-made alliances which Christ here dares us to break, some of the factors in this present life which have been joined and betrothed together by the will of heaven, and of which Christ says that we divorce them at our peril.

Take this, to begin with — *Religion and Character*. This is, beyond all doubt, one of these God-intended alliances. God has taken the two great facts — religion, that is, the inner life of the soul, and morality, that is, the outer life of conduct — and has declare it as His will that they should always go hand in hand. In other words, the only religion God wants to see, the only religion (to put it as bluntly as I can) for which God has any use, is a religion which is making a man good; and on the other hand, the only moral goodness which is secure is a goodness rooted firmly in religion. Religion and character — God has joined them together; and what God hath joined, let not man put asunder.

But man *has* put them asunder. That is the trouble. They may be theoretically inseparable: but in practice, how often they seem to lose touch, each pursuing its own alien way! Take an instance. Have you never known a man decidedly religious, zealous in piety to a marked degree, and yet singularly lacking in the love and joy and peace which, according to Paul, should be the fruit of the Spirit? You could not help feeling that, for any noticeable effect which it was having on his life, his religion might just as well not have been there at all. And on the other hand, have we not all known people — big-hearted, clean-living, utterly straightforward, amazingly attractive and lovable — and yet apparently able to dispense with religion and to stand aloof from its ordinances? That is the great perplexity, that religion and character, two entities bound together from the foundation of the world in a holy alliance and a God-intended unity, should so often in actual life be separated, and be seen going each on its own way with scarce a thought of the other. What God has joined, man has only too successfully sundered.

Take some illustrations which may help to make this clear — two from ancient history, and two from modern life.

Think of the ancient world as it was in the days when Israel suddenly emerged from the desert with the message of the one true God. We say that that world was heathen, but no one could possibly call it irreligious. It was almost too religious: there were altars on every high place, and shrines under every green tree. But morality — the sweetening, purifying, uplifting influence of religion upon character —

was scarcely to be found. On the contrary, here was religion (in some of its phases at least) degrading men, barbarising and dehumanising them, giving the animal in them free rein and sweeping them away on unchecked tides of passion — morality and religion, in other words, sundered as with the slash of some great Satanic sword.

Again, take the Mediterranean lands into which Paul carried the gospel of Jesus. 'Men of Athens,' cried the apostle on Mars' Hill, 'I perceive that in all things ye are *very religious*' — this, not 'too superstitious,' is the true translation. Shrines to every known god they had erected; and then, lest the claims of any deity should have been inadvertently overlooked, an altar 'To the Unknown God' was reared. The dominant religious influence in the Graeco-Roman world of this period was the so-called 'mystery cults' — strange, extravagent, Oriental ways of worship, which offered men salvation by playing upon their emotions. And when Paul came broadcasting through the Empire the glad tidings of Jesus Christ, and when converts began to pour into the Church, it was one of his biggest difficulties to compel them to realise that Jesus was not just a new emotional sensation like all these other deities, that the challenge of Jesus was directed at character and conduct, and that the man who thought he could accept Jesus as Lord and Master, and still go on living pretty much the same life he had been living before, did not know what he was saying. That is why, all through the epistles, you find Paul hammering at this fundamental fact, dinning it into their ears, that if they are really to call themselves Christ's men and women, then they must live in Christ's way; that, in short, the religion of Christ was in its very essence a morality.

But let us turn to two quite modern instances. Take the phenomenon which can be found flourishing in certain parts of Christendom today — a belief in what might be called 'mechanical grace'. You do certain actions. You perform certain rites. You observe certain rules. Then salvation is guaranteed. The real danger of such a belief is not its tincture of superstition, not even the fact that it is a regression to the pagan twilight from which Christ set us free: the real danger is that once you conceive of grace as operating mechanically and almost automatically, something which is sure to save a man, no matter the kind of life he leads, then obviously the incentive to personal moral strenuousness is gone. In other words, religion and morality are again put asunder.

At the opposite pole from this mechanical view of grace, and antagonistic to it in almost every respect — yet, curiously enough, often leading to the same unfortunate result of a divorce between religion and character — you have a certain type of over-simplified theology of salvation. You remember how, in Bunyan's dream, when pilgrim Christian was descending the hill where his burden had rolled away, he came upon three men lying fast asleep in the very shadow of the cross; and when he spoke to them, and tried to rouse them, they looked up drowsily for a moment, and called him a fool for his trouble, and lay down again in fancied security. Was not the cross there above their heads? And did not that cross guarantee everything? There is a religion like that. 'Jesus did it all,' it declares (which, thank God, is true); 'therefore there is nothing left for me to do.' But is that the authentic Gospel? Surely it is a far truer evangelicalism which says, 'Jesus did it all: therefore there is just everything for me to do!'

After all, what does it mean to be an evangelical? It means to believe in free grace and dying love and full atonement — and to believe in that with all the passion of your heart. But it does not mean to believe in these things in any way which blurs the fact that the Christian God is a holy God, that there is such a thing as the moral austerity of Christ, and that faith without works is dead.

Please do not misunderstand me. Take one of the greatest evangelical passages in Scripture. Take an instance of grace in action. Take Zacchaeus. Zacchaeus was 'soundly converted,' as we say. What happened then? Did Zacchaeus say, 'Jesus has done it all: there is nothing for me to do'? On the contrary! 'Jesus has done it all,' he said, 'and therefore there are a hundred things for me to do, and to do at once! I must start today. And the first thing is this — there has to be restitution to those people I have wronged. Lord,' he exclaimed, 'here is my resolve: if I have defrauded any man, I am going to seek him out, and make fourfold restoration.' In other words, when the man was saved, he proceeded immediately to face the moral consequences of being saved: he could not keep Christ's friendship on any other terms.

Does it not follow that a religion which leaves a man still liable to bursts of angry temper is lamentably incomplete; and that an experience of salvation which has not eradicated hardness, or self-seeking, or readiness to take offence is quite inadequate and scarce deserves the name? Jesus Himself made this abundantly plain. 'By their fruits ye shall know them,' He declared: by what they are in their home and in their business, by their life in the market and the club and the factory and the street, ye shall know — what? The worth of their religion! 'Not everyone that saith unto Me, "Lord, Lord," shall enter into the kingdom of heaven; but he that doeth the will of My Father.' There you have it — religion and character married together by God. And what God hath joined together, let not man put asunder.

Let us go on now, in the second place, to another God-made alliance which Christ warns us against breaking — *Faith and Reason*. Both faith and reason are gifts of God, wonderful and precious gifts; and it is quite certain that God always meant them to go hand in hand, and that only when they thus go hand in hand does man fulfil his destiny. But it is equally certain that again and again man has driven them apart.

There have been three great historic illustrations of this. When the Copernican theory, four hundred years ago, first startled the world, and men were compelled to adjust themselves to the discovery that their earth was not, as they had suppose, the fixed centre and hub of the universe, but only a planet like the others, revolving round the sun, the new theory was fiercely denounced. Faith and reason went to war over it; and bitter were the years of conflict before the resentment was overcome, and the truth was received, and faith and reason consented to join hands. Again, at a later time, when the researches of geology had put the age of the earth, not at a few modest thousand years, but at a figure reckoned in many millions, the loud protesting voices were heard, and the war broke out once more. But there, too, the truth established itself, and faith and reason were reconciled. Finally, in the middle of last century, when modern science entered the field, the cry was raised again that the very foundations of the faith were being undermined, and that this was a dethroning of God: and it took a generation and more to quell that fear, and to bring the new truth into its own.

How does the matter stand today? We are living in an age when man has seen the mental furniture of his house of life radically overhauled — much old lumber cast away, and many new thought-forms incorporated — and all this in the shortest conceivable time. The new generation has to set all its experiences and hopes and aspirations against a vastly altered background. What is the attitude of evangelical religion to this situation? That question is being raised both outside the Churches and within; and we should be failing in a clear duty if we refused to face it. But the answer, surely, is quite simple and definite. It is this: evangelical religion, by its very nature, cannot countenance the putting asunder of things which God has joined together. It has no desire to see faith and reason divorced. If only that were realised! I will go further, and point out that evangelical religion has three propositions to urge against any such separation.

The first is, that it is so unnecessary. You will recall the old story of Uzzah, the timid, well-meaning soul, who trembled for the ark of the Lord, and put out his hand to steady it, and fell stricken to the earth for his presumption. Don't think the ark of God requires protecting! Don't think the gospel truth needs any of our nervous expedients. Don't try to shelter Christ from the challenge of the world. He can stand where the light is fiercest, can stand with the search-light of all man's latest knowledge beating upon Him, and survive by His own inherent strength — and not only sur-vive, but draw souls to Himself by the ten thousand! Look back across the past, and tell me — has Christ been weak-ened by any of those discoveries of reason which were at first so bitterly resented? The old belief in a fixed earth as the centre of everything — has Christianity been hurt because we do not accept that any longer? The pushing back of the earth's age to an unimaginable antiquity — has that robbed us of one iota of the living gospel of Christ? The advance of modern science — has that really, as some timid souls feared, shaken down the throne of providence? Why, it has given us a far mightier conception of providence, a far more majestic thought of God, and a far deeper meaning in our own life struggle, than we had ever envisaged before! Do not let us sunder faith and reason then: it is so un-necessary.

But evangelical religion goes further. Such a separation, it declares, is not only unnecessary: it is definitely wrong. When Jesus said, 'Thou shalt love the Lord thy God with all thy mind,' He implied that anything in religion which even suggested tampering with the truth or shutting out the light would be downright sin. It is a terribly significant fact that it was the closed and shuttered mind, the refusal to welcome new light, in other words, the breach between tradition and truth, which was the sin of the New Testament

Pharisees; and when Jesus went to His death at their hands, it was in protest against that breach, and to heal that breach, that He died.

One further step evangelical religion takes. To put faith and reason apart, it declares, is not only unnecessary and wrong: practically it is disastrous. Any faith that is frightened has already lost the battle of the future. There is a story in the annals of the British Navy which tells that on one occasion a destroyer was lying in a harbour of the West Indies, where five other ships of various nationalities were anchored. Suddenly a furious storm descended, with a wild, terrifying wind, and great waves sweeping right into the harbour. What did the British captain do? He weighed anchor, and steamed straight out to sea, in the very teeth of the storm. Two days later he returned, battered but safe; and there were the other five ships lying piled up, wrecked upon the foreshore. It was their very refusal to face the seas and the storm, their clinging to security, which had been their undoing. Only the ship that ventured everything came through. And a faith today which, dreading risk and danger, clung to the old securities and shunned the light of knowledge and advancing truth, would be courting disaster. The future is with the faith that dares. For here are faith and and reason, welded together by the will of God Almighty. And what God hath joined together, let not man put asunder. That is evangelical freedom. Stand fast therefore in the liberty wherewith Christ has made you free!

But now I want to turn your thoughts in closing to a third of these God-made alliances we find in life. This is the greatest of them all. It is *the Human Soul and Jesus*. Has not God joined these together, intending them from all eternity for each other — the soul of a man and Christ? Yes, deep down in every heart that lives, even in the poorest and shabbiest and most sinful, there is an instinctive kinship with the Man of Nazareth. This kinship is the world's one hope; and it is God's doing, who at Bethlehem brought the human soul and Jesus very near, and at Calvary betrothed them together for ever and for ever.

And therefore — for this follows inevitably — it is a terrible thing for any man to put one soul and Jesus asunder, terrible to do anything by word or deed or example which may slacken some one's hold on truth and purity, terrible to blot out the shining of Jesus' face for one of His little ones.

Do we say there is no chance that we should ever do that? Let us not be too sure. For every time our witness to the Master breaks down, every time we weakly give temptation the right of way through our own lives, we are dimming the reality of God for someone else, and blurring the face of Jesus for some one who had been hoping to see Him clearly.

But if that is bad, what shall we say about the man who deliberately plays the tempter to another soul? The man who sows the first unclean thought in an innocent mind, or laughs away the scrupulous pieties that some young life has learned at home, or turns some defenceless trust to bitterness — what shall we say of him? Anything we like: but here is what the Word declares — that that man, the offender of one of God's little ones, is God's enemy, and the blood of the slain will God yet require at his hand.

What God hath joined together — the human soul and Jesus — let not man put asunder! That is the terror of it. But this, on the other side, is the glorious thrilling joy of it, that it is in the power of everyone of us to go out and find some other life which has never known Jesus yet, or which having once known Him, has been separated from Him again — to go out and get hold of such a soul and bring it where Jesus is; and then (think of it, the glory and joy of it!) to take that soul's right hand, and to take the Lord Christ's right hand, and to bring these two right hands together, clasping each other, and so to betroth them to each other — that soul and

Jesus — with troth plighted until death and beyond! It is in your power and mine, that amazing opportunity: and it ought to make us glad that we are alive.

My last word must be this. Is there some one here today still on the quest for Christ? Someone looking wistfully towards religion, and longing for assurance, and yet feeling that He is so dim, this Christ, so vague and very far away? Some one perhaps losing hope of ever finding Him, or of gaining a real experience of His presence and His love?

My friend, let me tell you now: *God has made Christ and you for each other*. He made the gospel of Christ to suit your very need. Do not hesitate. Get hold of Jesus by any point you can. If it is the teaching of Jesus that appeals to you, get hold of Him by that. If it is His grace or winsomeness or valour, get hold of Him by that. If it is His tenderness, get hold of Him by that. If it is the amazing death He died, get hold of Him by that. It does not matter where you grasp Him for a beginning, so long as you do get hold of Him. You are meant for each other, you and Jesus. Give Him your love and loyalty now: and those whom God thus joins together — your soul and Jesus — nothing, no, not death itself when death comes to you one day, shall ever put asunder.

XV

Our Worries and Christ's Peace

'Peace I leave with you, My peace I give unto you.'
— JOHN xiv. 27.

THIS WAS CHRIST'S LAST WILL AND TESTAMENT. THIS WAS His only legacy. He had nothing else to leave. He was the poorest of the poor. He had no material posessions of any kind to divide amongst the men He loved. So He bequeathed to them the one thing which was in His power to give. He gave His peace.

But could there have been a more priceless possession than just that? Never a congregation meets for worship but some are there who are needing more than anything else to learn the secret of a true serenity. 'Never morning wore to evening, but some heart did break' for lack of the very thing which Christ is so eager to bestow. I fancy there must be few in this House of God this morning who have never prayed, out of the depths of personal experience, some such prayer as Whittier's:

'Take from our souls the strain and stress,
And let our ordered lives confess
The beauty of Thy peace.'

Now I think you will agree with me that part at least of the blame for the shortage of serenity which characterises modern life must be laid at the door of the age in which we are living. It is certainly not easy to achieve inner peace today, or to maintain it unbroken against the assaults and invasions of this untranquil world. And if more people now than ever before are highly strung and nervously irritable and lacking in repose, that is not surprising. For the general insecurity of the present time registers itself not only politically and economically: the toll it takes emotionally and mentally is no whit less serious.

What burdens men and women are carrying! Do you think peace can come easily to a man who is out of work? Or to his wife, trying desperately to make ends meet in the home? Or to tired folk, overdriven almost to the breaking-point? Or to parents wondering about careers for their children? Or to lonely souls who feel that this bustling world does not need them nor want them, and that they are no use at all to anyone? The age in which we are living must accept much of the responsibility for strained faces and lives that have lost their peace.

But not all. The real trouble lies deeper. Look into your own heart. Explore the causes of your own restless moods and feelings. Talk to your soul about that sense of strain. Can you say, 'It is not my fault: it is circumstances that are to blame'? No. If we are honest with ourselves, we know that will not do. Let us ask ourselves some questions Why do we ever grow irritable? Why do our nerves get on edge, so that we say things we regret the moment afterwards? Why do we try to cross bridges before we come to them? Why do we find it difficult to relax? Why are there those days when nothing will go right, when work is a burden, and people are exasperating, and life is all worry and fret? Shall we blame the world for that? Surely the trouble is in ourselves. One thing we lack — the peace of Christ, His last and greatest gift.

Would you like peace today? I do not mean the peace of lethargic ease or of a safe and sheltered life. Nor do I mean the peace of the emotionless Stoic, who achieves calm by doing violence to his affections, and by damping down the fires of love and sorrow and pity in his heart. I do not mean that. I mean the peace that stands sentinel at the gateway of the soul, and confronts all manner of difficult things with steady eyes, the peace that holds the heart serene through crowded days and overwork and all the criticisms of men. Would you like that? Well, says the Gospel, you can have it. It is not a matter of temperament: the most highly strung soul can have it. It is a matter of accepting a gift. 'My peace I give unto you,' said Jesus.

Notice His language. '*My* peace.' The peace that My heart knows. Will you think of that? Jesus did not often speak about it, but on every page of the Gospels you can feel it.

The serenity of Christ! Look at the narratives. Did anyone, watching Jesus in those Galilean days, ever see Him irritated? Think what He had to put up with. Could you have stood it and remained serene? Continual intrusions upon His privacy, no respite from dawn to dark, the steady drain on His spiritual resources, inconsiderate people breaking in on His hours of quiet, the awful burden of sharing every hurt heart's sins and sorrows and of feeling them as personally as if they were His own, the misunderstandings, the cutting criticisms, the pettiness of people, the terrible, unremitting toil, the disappointments, the crushing load of such a life — and yet, through it all, that same serene, untroubled heart. No flurry, no sign of strain upon His face, no trace of nerves — always 'My peace'. Is there anything more marvellous in the Gospels than just that?

Contrast His own disciples. Their nerves sometimes gave way. There was a Samaritan village that was rude and inhospitable. 'Lord,' they cried exasperated, 'let us call down fire from heaven! Let us teach these boorish folk a lesson.' But Jesus? 'Ye know not what manner of spirit ye are of.' Always that strong serenity! The frail boat was being tossed, one night on a murderous sea. 'Master,' they shouted, all self-control flung to the winds, 'Master, carest Thou not that we perish?' 'Peace, be still,' said Jesus, and I think He was speaking to those panic-stricken hearts as much as to the angry waves, 'Peace, be still.' Always that inner calm. A crowd of five thousand people followed them one day out to their secret retreat in the wilderness. 'Send them away,' said the disciples, 'for heaven's sake, let us have a holiday for once!' 'They need not depart,' said Jesus, 'they are sheep without a shepherd, and I love them.' Always that heart at leisure from itself. Then came the end; and things went terribly wrong, or so it seemed. 'Don't go to Jerusalem,' they implore Him, 'there is danger in the air —don't go!' And when He went, and the enemy struck, their strained nerves snapped completely: they all turned and fled. But Jesus? 'Father, into Thy hands I commend My Spirit.' And so He died serene. Is it not marvellous? All the way from Bethlemen to Nazareth, and from Nazareth to Calvary — 'My peace', My strong, untroubled peace!

'Ah,' you say, 'but that was Jesus! He was different. We are common clay. You can't expect us to achieve that poise of soul, that spirit serene. It was lovely, it was marvellous, it was magnificent: but for us — utterly and for ever impossible!'

I beg you not to be too sure of that. If I could today convince one troubled heart that this thing — the peace of Christ, which is the peace of God that passeth understanding — is not a far-off dream, but actually within reach of anyone who will claim it; if even one person were to go away from this church this morning quite sure of this, that whatever life may do, there is always far more in Jesus to hold a man steady and serene than there can be anywhere else in life to shake or unnerve his soul — our service would not have been in vain.

For the real marvel is not only to hear, all through the story of Jesus from the carpenter's bench to the cross, the deep central theme, 'My peace': the real marvel is to hear Him saying, as I believe He is saying now, 'My peace I give *to you*' — to you who know what it means to be rushed and fretted and agitated and worried: 'My peace — to you!'

How does it come? Well, the way to answer that is to ask, How did it come to Jesus? What was the secret of His serenity?

We have seen already what it was not. It was neither the cheap serenity of a sheltered existence, nor the barren serenity of a Stoic philosophy. What was it, then?

I think Christ's peace was, first, *the peace of adequate resources*. There can be few things more wearing to the nerves than to face life, or to face some task in life, with deficient spiritual resources. 'That is the real curse of Adam,' wrote C. E. Montague, 'not the work in itself, but the worry and doubt of ever getting it done.' How many there are who know that feeling! The consciousness of inadequate resources can almost drive a man distracted It can give him sleepless nights. It can keep him perpetually on the strain. It can weigh upon him until he is utterly miserable. But there was nothing of that with Jesus. He moved from one task to another without halting and without haste. He never had the haggard look of one who has reached his limit. He spent Himself without stint, but there was always more behind it and within. And so He was free from the fret and care that lay waste so many lesser souls. The peace of Christ was the peace of a supreme adequacy for life.

Now He can give you that. He can give you adequate resources for every duty life can lay upon you, for the fearsome responsibilities you would like to run away from, for the crowded days when the pressure of work is becoming a nightmare, for the hours of crisis that take you unawares. He can make you more than equal to this difficult, puzzling life. He can give you — if only you will open your heart to the gift — His Holy Spirit. That is the supreme resource. That is the final adequacy. And to realise it is to find life and healing. To possess it is enduring peace.

Notice, second, that the peace of Christ was *the peace of a disciplined life*. Here, I think, is a discovery we all make sooner or later, that slackness of any kind — whether in work, or thought, or life — is always destructive of inner repose. Restlessness and unhappiness are the inevitable nemesis of the life of passing whim and purposeless drift. Wordsworth put that well:

> 'Me this unchartered freedom tires;
> I feel the weight of chance desires:
>
> .   .   .   .   .   .
>
> I long for a repose that ever is the same.'

But whenever you see, shining on the face of some man or some woman whom you meet, the radiance of a deep inner serenity, you may safely say, 'There has been discipline there — discipline of time, discipline of thought, discipline of heart's desire!' The peace of Christ was the peace of a disciplined life. And if on these terms you will receive it — 'My peace I give unto you.'

Now that brings to light a third element in the Master's secret. The peace of Christ was *the peace of a clean heart*. It does not matter much how difficult life may be, as long as the conscience is at rest. The real wreckers of peace — what are they? Not any of the slings and arrows of disappointed hopes. No. But memories that sting because of sins still unforgiven, the remorse that cries down the winds of the passing days, 'Thou art the man,' the divided loyalties that strike an uneasy bargain between the vision of God and the lure of the world, the breakdown of goodwill and love, the resentments that brood in secret, the jealousies that torture the mind, the temptations never seriously resisted — these are the real wreckers, destroying all peace of soul. But — O Christ of God, how pure you were, how consistent and untainted! Yours was the peace of a heart forever clean. And again, on these terms, His offer stands: 'My peace I give unto you.'

One thing alone remains. The peace of Christ was the peace of adequate resources, of a disciplined life, and of a clean heart. Notice, finally, that it was *the peace of fellowship with God.* This is the ultimate secret. I see Jesus in the Gospels slipping away from the clamorous crowds when night descends. Where is He going? He is going to some lonely garden, to rest His weary soul on God. I see Him stealing out of the house at Bethany long before dawn is in the sky, and while the village is still asleep. Where is He making for? He is seeking the secret trysting-place, where He has pledged to meet His Father. I see Him entering a city's streets where multitudes of hurt and ailing creatures wait hopefully for His coming — I see Him no longer weary as on the night before, but travelling to meet that crowded day in the greatness of His strength, mighty to save. Where has He been? He has been on the mountain-top, laying that day and all its work before God in prayer, and receiving help and power. And seeing that, I know that I have found the final secret. The peace of Christ was the peace of perfect fellowship with God.

'My peace I give unto you.' Will you accept it? Will you make room and space in your life for that fellowship with God without which it cannot come? Will you do what God has perhaps been waiting for years for some of us to do — stop thinking that you have to carry alone that burden of work, that harassing problem, and cast your burden on the Lord? It is never a waste of time, in the morning, or at midday, or in the evening, to thrust aside — for five minutes, ten minutes, an hour if you like — the insistent, pressing cares, and to be still and remember God. If you would only believe that the time thus diverted from ordinary things would more than repay you by the pose and steadiness which you would carry back to life from that secret place of the Most High!

For that is fact. To have daily fellowship with God through Jesus is to have found the peace which nothing in life, not all the trials and vexations in the world, can ever take away.

> 'Dear! of all happy in the hour, most blest
>   He who has found our hid security.
> We have built a house that is not for Time's throwing,
>   We have gained a peace unshaken by pain for ever.'

Joseph Conrad, in an essay, quotes from a letter of Sir Robert Stopford. Stopford was one of Nelson's men. He was commander of one of the ships with which Nelson chased to the West Indies a fleet nearly double in number. And describing the experiences and hardships of that desperate adventure, Stopford wrote the words: 'We are half-starved, and otherwise inconvenienced by being so long out of port. But our reward is — we are with Nelson!'

My brother, my sister, life may prove harsh and difficult enough, may deny your dreams and half starve your hopes; but if you can say, 'I am with Christ, and through Christ with God,' you have your reward. You have found on earth the very peace of heaven.

XVI

The Word and Will of the Lord

'Now in the fifteenth year of the reign of Tiberius
Caesar, Pontius Pilate being governor of Judea . . . the
word of God came unto John . . . in the wilderness.'
— LUKE iii. 1, 2.

NO ONE WHO READS THE FOUR GOSPELS WITH ANY
discernment can fail to observe that the third has a character
all its own. Even if nothing had been known about the
various writers — their names or nationality or antecedents
— we could have guessed, from internal evidence alone,
that the third evangelist unlike the others, was of Gentile
and not Jewish extraction.

In point of fact, we know that Matthew, Mark, and John
were Jews born and bred, with Semitic blood in their veins,
and a Hebrew outlook upon life. Luke alone was a Greek, a
citizen of the wider world. And that fact has coloured every
page he wrote. The mark of this Gospel is its catholicity,
its internationalism, its passionate emphasis on *the world-
significance of Jesus.*

One or two illustrations will suffice to make this clear.

It is noteworthy that Matthew, in tracing Jesus' ancestry,
starts from Abraham, the founder of Israel. But Luke's
genealogy of Jesus lifts the whole matter out of that narrower
and purely nationalist setting, and runs back to Adam, the
founder of the race, and beyond Adam to God Himself, the
Father of all mankind: 'the son of Adam, the son of God'
is how the genealogy ends.

Moreover, the fact that Luke, in his opening verses, dedicates his work to Theophilus — 'most excellent Theophilus,' he calls him, or as we should put it, 'your Excellency,' which indicates that Theophilus was some high official of the Imperial Roman Government and probably not a Christian — that fact prepares us at the outset for a narrative in which the missionary interest will be supreme, and the world-significance of the Gospel will predominate over its purely local Palestinian reference.

Matthew, working with his Jewish background, sees Jesus primarily as the Messiah of the Jews, and the fulfilment of Old Testament prophecy. This was only natural. But Luke, with his more cosmopolitan horizons, sees Jesus as the Saviour of humanity. Witness the place which his narrative gives to the Samaritans, whom the Jews despised: Luke alone records the parable of the Good Samaritan, and the incident of the one grateful leper ('and he was a Samaritan') Witness, too, the parable of the Prodigal Son — which Luke alone preserves — a story which almost certainly carries a universal as well as an individual reference, the younger brother whom the father welcomed home so eagerly standing for the irreligious Gentile world in all its sin and need, and the elder brother who repulsed him representing the Jewish. In short, the key-note of this Gospel is its universalism.

Now in the light of this, read again the evangelist's prologue to the drama of redemption. Notice the curiously elaborate historical approach which he employs. 'In the fifteenth year of the reign of Tiberius Caesar, Pontius Pilate being governor of Judaea, and Herod being tetrarch of Galilee and his brother Philip tetrarch of Ituraea, and of the region of Trachonitis, and Lysanias the tetrarch of Abilene, Annas and Caiaphas being the high priests, the word of God came unto John the son of Zacharias in the wilderness.'

Why is the man so careful about his history? Why this laborious linking up with world-events? It is his way of asserting the world-relevance of Christ. There, he says in effect, was the scene upon which Christianity launched itself. There was the world-stage into which the religion of Jesus came. There was the panorama — kings and governors, principalities and powers, imperial policies, movements of history, currents of feeling and thought — into which there suddenly marched — *God*! You will miss the whole point of the story I am going to tell, says Luke, unless you see that world-panorama as the background to the message of the Christ.

Now see the force of this for us today. There is a spirit in the present age that would politely bow religion into a corner. Christianity, on this view, is a purely private concern. The Christian experience of the individual carries no external authority whatever. If a man chooses to be religious, let him be — it is his own affair. If people want to go to church, let them go — it is a harmless indulgence. If some misguided creatures persist in regarding the Sermon on the Mount as practical politics, let them so regard it — the world knows better.

So speaks the spirit of the age. If you must have religion, pray keep it in its place. Remember that it is just your personal opinion, after all. And remember that, as such, it is purely subjective, a private sentiment, a species of aesthetic indulgence, with no objective validity. It has no authority to speak on matters like race relationships, or the colour question, or war and peace, or slum housing, or the human factor in industry. Keep your religion where it belongs: we want no intrusion or interference! So speaks a prevalent temper of the age.

But that is the very spirit to which Luke here throws down the gauntlet unmistakably, setting religion in the framework of world-events, and by so doing proclaiming the truth that Christianity is not a private indulgence of a few religious folk: it is the very Mind and Programme of God for the race, a Mind and Programme which humanity must ultimately reckon with and embrace, or else — go out into the night forever.

Notice further, how dramatically the evangelist, in his prologue, has brought out *the contrast between the passing and the permanent*. 'In the fifteenth year of the reign of Tiberius Caesar, Pontius Pilate being governor of Judaea,' and so on, 'the word of God came unto John in the wilderness.' Is it not surprising? The sentence which begins with the roll of these great and mighty names — the Caesars, the wind of whose terrible power had swept to the ultimate seas, the governors and tetrarchs beneath whose eminence and majesty and dignity the common world bowed and trembled — the sentence ends (surely a dreadful bathos, a startling anti-climax!) with the name of a penniless preacher of the desert.

If you were reading this for the first time, you might well ask, What is he doing in that company? What possible connection can there be between these great, exalted personages marching across the page of history, and this poor, insignificant hermit of the desert wastes? What is the use of mentioning them in the same breath at all?

Tell Tiberius Caesar, yonder amid the plaudits of his Senate, that a queer, hungry-looking evangelist has appeared in a remote corner of his dominions. 'And what is the interest of that to me?' Tiberius will say. 'You must surely see I have not the fraction of a moment of my time to spare for trivialities like that!' Tell Pilate, Herod, and Lysanias that there is someone yonder at the Jordan babbling about having received a word from God, and see how pityingly they will look at you. 'What is that to us? Are we to take cognizance of every prating fool who rises?'

But what, Tiberius, if we have to tell you that the lonely evangelist with the name of John will be a hero and a household word to millions and a shining light of men, long after your proud name and memory are but the merest blur on history's page? And Pilate, Herod, and Lysanias, what if we have to tell you that your names would never have been mentioned in history at all, not one of them, that you would never have been heard of by posterity, had it not been for your connection — your strange and brief and discreditable connection — with the cause of which this same John was the herald?

For that is the truth. 'In the fifteenth year of the reign of Caesar, in the governorship of Pontius Pilate' — how solid and influential and enduring it seemed, that drama of the nations — 'the word of God came to John in the wilderness' — how trivial and evanescent, by comparison, that! But history itself has given the verdict. Tiberius, Pilate, Herod, Lysanias, and all their pomp and might — mere foam on the face of time's hurrying stream: but John, the called of God, standing foursquare still to the winds of the centuries, standing like that very Rock of Ages to whom all his words bore witness!

What a contrast it is between the passing and the permanent; between lives that go out like a candle when they are done, because all along they have been fundamentally godless, with nothing spiritual and therefore nothing lasting about them, and lives that go marching on deathlessly for ever, because they are eternal with the very eternity of God!

This is what persecutors in every age have failed to realise. They have smothered idealism, outlawed religion, trampled righteousness underfoot. They have stoned their Stephens, burnt their Latimers, drowned their Margaret Wilsons. They have crucified their Christ. They have come down the slopes of Calvary, when it was over, congratulating themselves on their achievement. 'That is the end of you, Jesus! You will never trouble us again.'

Never? 'The blood of the martyrs is the seed of the

Church.' And those who strike the weak things of this world, which are Christ's, find sooner or later that they have struck rock, sheer granite!

'The world passeth away,' said an apostle, 'and the lust thereof' — and that means the reckless ambitions thereof, the cruel tyrannies and the megalomania and the pomp and pride thereof, 'it passeth away,' and the men who take that line flicker out and cease: 'but he that doeth the will of God abideth forever.'

And to bring this nearer home, we ask, How does it stand within our own souls? If some things in this world are passing, and other things are permanent, then clearly the vital question is, To which are we linking up our lives? With which are we secretly identified in our inmost hearts? In that question lies our destiny. Link yourself to the things that perish — the materialisms, the selfishnesses, the earthly pleasures which go out at last into the dark — link yourself to them, and your doom is to go out with them. But link yourself to the things that remain — the righteousness that is of God, the purity that guards the vision, the unselfish love that only thinks of others — link yourself to these, and to the Christ in whom they have reached their crowning glory, and your destiny is to survive the stars themselves, and to stand even on the day when God sweeps the world away.

> 'Saviour, if of Zion's city
>   I, through grace a member am,
> Let the world deride or pity,
>   I will glory in Thy Name.
> Fading is the worldling's pleasure,
>   All his boasted pomp and show;
> Solid joys and lasting treasure
>   None but Zion's children know.'

Here then, in Luke's prologue, we have discovered, first,

a passionate assertion of the world-significance of Christianity, and second, a vivid contrast of the passing and the permanent. Will you notice now, finally, that we have here *a dramatic description of the dawning of a soul*? 'The Word of God came to John in the wilderness.'

What does it mean, this phrase which is used of all the great prophet souls of Scripture at the opening of their ministry — 'The Word of the Lord came' to him? Does it mean some sort of magic? Does it hint that these men were in some way psychically abnormal and unbalanced? Was it all perhaps auto-suggestion? Did they simply imagine and invent things, and then dignify their own fancies with the name of deity? No, it means nothing like that. It means exactly what it says. It means that God, who after all is the living God, and therefore presumably able to speak, had actually spoken to them. It means that into their long brooding on righteousness, temperance, and judgment to come, there had flashed a light from heaven, there had broken a voice more ringing and authentic than any of the voices of the world; and so they stood and cried, 'We have seen, and heard — and know. Thus saith the Lord!'

It means — but why should I describe it thus impersonally? It means what has happened to some of you here — was it perhaps at a First Communion when you suddenly knew Christ mattered more than anything? Or in a day of difficult decision, when rival paths confronted you, and then the way of duty leapt to clearness before you, and you knew you had to take that way, or else never be able to look Christ your Lord in the face again? Or in an hour of temptation, when moral issues had grown blurred and been forgotten, and the inner citadel was in danger, and then, like a bugle-call across the ramparts of your soul, there spoke a voice — 'That is wrong'; and you knew that this was no mere personal scruple which was intervening, but the authentic challenge of the universe, the voice of the God of your salvation? 'Or was it on some day when the darkness and the bitterness of this confused and disappointing world were lying like a deadly blight upon your spirit, and then suddenly one truth grew luminous — the truth that, whatever happens, it is better to be honest than to be false, better to be clean than to be unclean — so that in that moment you would have been glad to die for your conviction? Then, by whatever way the experience has come, you know what the evangelist here is meaning. You have shared in this drama of a dawning soul. And you can take John the Baptist's name out of it, and insert your own. 'The word of the Lord came unto me.'

Have you not heard it? If ever you have been conscious of Someone coming to meet you when you prayed; if you have ever felt the sudden pressure of an unseen will coming into contact with your own, to challenge or to sustain; if ever music, or the glory of a sunset, or the first flowers of springtime, or a deed of unexpected kindness, or the sight of a pure and lovely face, or some haunting word of Jesus Christ has opened a sudden window in your soul towards absolute reality; if you have ever felt a wave of sickening shame for something wrong you had done; if you have ever risen from your knees a different man; if you have ever sacrificed yourself for some one, in a way which the cold logic of common-sense thought unreasonable, and yet somehow you just had to do it — do you know what that experience was? It was God giving you a glimpse of Himself. It was life for a moment becoming sacramental. It was a revelation of the unseen order, the absolute, eternal reality behind things seen and temporal. It was the word of the Lord to you.

But why does it not come more often? And why does it not come to every one without exception — this voice of the Lord God Almighty? Why are so many still stubbornly denying that God declares His mind at all, still doggedly asserting — 'No word of the Lord has ever come to me: all your notions of a divine, guiding voice are myth and make-believe'? Why?

It is because our modern life is so noisy, and the press and jostle of a thousand cares and duties so blatant and so deafening. What chance is there, amid all that, to hear the one still, small voice which matters most of all?

The Baptist's world was noisy too — Roman legions marching up and down the land, the endless babble of the marketplace, the clash of political opinions, voices loud and passionate, voices fierce and hectoring and God-denying — it was a chaotic medley of a world when the gospel day was born. But see what the writer says: 'The word of God came unto John *in the wilderness*.' Here was a man who had made a space in which his half-suffocated soul could breathe, had made a silence in which his half-deafened soul could be at peace and listen: and it was then he heard God speaking!

Does someone protest — 'But that is foolish, for we can't cut the cables that bind us to our appointed lot: we can't take the wings of the morning, and hie away to some peaceful patch of desert'? Ah, that is not the point. 'I pray not that Thou shouldest take them out of the world,' said Jesus. But where is the man who cannot have ten minutes of silence in his life each day, to put it near the barest minimum, ten minutes to draw his soul into the healing silence of the eternal, with the world barred out, and to hear what God the Lord will speak? You can do it — and you know it. And if any of us has ceased doing it, he can start again today — and he knows it.

How terribly much we stand to lose if God's precious life-giving words, when they fall athwart our souls, find us — through our refusal of the way of prayer — deaf as the stones of the street! And how gloriously and magnificently much we gain when our lives are tuned in daily to the voice of the eternal!

It is the one thing needful. O for a closer walk with God!

XVII

If Christ Be Not Risen!

> 'If Christ be not raised, your faith is vain; ye are yet in your sins. Then they also which are fallen asleep in Christ are perished. ... But now is Christ risen from the dead.' — 1 Cor. xv. 17, 18, 20.

ONE OF THE MOST PATHETIC SENTENCES EVER SPOKEN BY human lips came, surprisingly enough, from a hard, cold-blooded, cynical Roman. He was a man who had power and was proud of it. He had been commissioned to maintain the dignity of empire and the might of Caesar among a conquered people. Not the type of man you can readily imagine becoming pathetic! His name was Pontius Pilate. On the day in question, his subordinates and advisers were worried and uneasy. They were badgering him about the necessity of doing something — now that Jesus was dead and buried and finished and put away in the tomb — to make sure that there would be no tricks at the grave, no rifling of the sepulchre, no concocting of tales by His friends to the effect that He was not dead. 'You must do something, Pilate,' they said, 'you must take precautions.' And so it came, this most pathetic sentence ever spoken. 'Ye have a watch,' said Pilate, 'go your way, make the tomb as sure as ye can.'

If you were to see a man going out in the grey of the dawn and shouting to the sun, 'Stop! You shan't climb the heavens today!' or if you saw him, when the tide had ebbed and had begun to return, standing on the shore, drawing a line in the sand, and then crying to the waves that were heaving their shoulders for a new advance, 'Halt! You shan't pass the line!' — what would you say of him? You would say the man was mad. What, then, will you say of this pathetic Roman who thought he could barricade the tomb of God?

But wait! It is Eastertide again. *Is this thing true?* This victory, this miracle, this Resurrection — did it happen? If — ah, if — by any chance — we have been mistaken, off the track, deluded! If Pilate perhaps was not quite so pathetic after all! If — Jesus — never —— 'Oh, stop,' says someone. 'Don't think of it! Don't mention it. It makes us shudder. It is a dismal, horrible, hideous idea!' I know. But what if it is Christ, speaking through His apostle here, who compels us to think of it? 'If Christ be not risen,' he says — forcing that upon us.

I know there is a shudder in it. John Henry Newman has a memorable passage in which he imagines what it would feel like to look out into the world and see no trace of God at all. That would be, he says, 'just as if I were to look into a mirror and not see my face.' Think of it — that sudden, almost terrifying suggestion — looking straight into a mirror and seeing only a blank! It is that same shudder of the soul that Paul's words here create —'If Christ be not risen.'

Or think of this. Suppose that one day this earth were suddenly to break out of its own orbit, were not to go circling round the sun any more, but were to fly off at a tangent, farther and farther away out into the cold immensities of space; and men waited wonderingly for the coming of the spring and it never came, waited with weariness for the birds return and the buds on the trees, and there was never a sign of it, only deeper and ever deeper winter; and they said, 'Surely tomorrow it will come! We'll wake tomorrow to a breath of springtime!' — and still nothing happened — no spring, no summer, but only that deathly coldness gripping the earth as it whirled farther and farther away; until at last the truth broke on them, and there was a great, bitter cry — 'We are doomed!' It is the same wild shudder of the soul that meets you here — 'If Christ be not risen.'

'Don't think of it!' we say. 'But,' answers Paul, 'you must! You have to look this in the face. Else your belief is just a coward belief.' Here Paul himself looks it in the face, and compels those Corinthians to do it. You can picture the congregation in Corinth that Sunday when the apostle's letter to them arrived and was read aloud in their hearing; you can see something passing over them like a wind over a field of corn — that swift, nameless shudder. Challengingly, bluntly, Paul sets it down; and then goes on to draw the consequences. 'If Christ be not risen' — what then? Three things. And it is these we are to consider now.

First, this. 'If Christ be not risen, *your faith is vain.*' All the trust you have ever put in God — one huge mistake! All the brave confidence you have cherished — smashed, torn to shreds, blown into thin air! Your faith in God is gone, finished.

Now why? Why is that involved in it? Ah, you can see why. For here was Jesus, who had lived an absolutely perfect life — crucified, dead, buried, and that was all! Here was Jesus, who all His life long had trusted that God would deliver Him, that God would 'not leave His soul in hell, nor suffer His Holy One to see corruption' — and God did nothing. You can't trust God after that, says Paul, neither His love, nor His power.

You can't trust His love. There is a woman in Mary Webb's story *Precious Bane*, a poor woman with a huge heart of love; and one day — 'It always seemed a strange thing to me,' she exclaims, 'that the mother of Jesus could keep her hands off the centurion, and it could only have been because her Son had given orders afore. But indeed if it had been me, I think I should have forgot the orders.' If human love can feel like that about it, is it not strange that God, watching the tragedy on Golgotha, should have done nothing? Long ago someone read the story of the death of

Jesus to King Clovis, who was a barbarian, not a Christian; and suddenly, as the story went on, his hand reached for his sword, and drew it, and 'Oh,' he cried, 'if only I had been there with my Franks! We'd have charged up the slopes of Calvary, and smashed those Romans, and saved Him!' But if God, watching Calvary, did nothing — left it at that, and knew this was the end of Christ for ever? Then we are back where Huxley was. 'I cannot see,' he said 'one shadow or tittle of evidence that God is love.' Your faith is vain.

Moreover, you can't trust His power. For the clash you see at Calvary was not only between Jesus and His enemies: it was between God and the devil — the two great world-powers grappling there, locked in wrestler's grip. And if the cross finished things, then down in the underworld that night there must have rung a savage cry, 'We win! We win! God is blotted out.' Power? says Paul. If Christ be not raised, don't tell me God is power. Your faith is vain.

Well, does it matter? For us? Is our faith in God such an important thing that it would matter to us to lose it? Would it make any difference? Perhaps in some moods we think not. Our faith is not much of an asset. We are rather vague and indefinite about it. It is not all-important. Perhaps we think that. But I know this, that if that faith of yours were one day threatened with extinction, if life wanted to take it away, you would be on your feet in a moment, crying, 'No! Leave that! Anything else you like, but for God's sake leave me that!'

It does matter. You cannot live without it. There was a great German who drew a terrible, imaginative picture of Jesus returning to earth and confessing that all His teaching about God had been mistaken, that He had discovered there was no Father God behind things after all, and that He had thought it best to come back and tell men so; and all the world, hearing that, was broken down into tears. It does matter. You can't live without it. And if Christ be not raised, it is gone.

But if Christ be risen from the dead — ah, then faith in God is crowned, justified, vindicated! Then, in the blackest days, your life is safe knowing that the God who did *that* will assuredly see you through. Then you can sing your Magnificat, like those priests in Alsace in the War who sang it through the crash of bursting shells. 'Tell me,' said one of Luther's enemies to him sneeringly, 'tell me — when the whole world turns against you — Church, State, princes, people — where will you be then?' 'Where shall I be then?' cried the great soul. 'Why, then as now, in the hands of Almighty God!' And if Christ be raised from the dead, you and I can be Luthers too.

> 'Let troubles rise and terrors frown,
>   And days of darkness fall;
> Through Him all dangers we'll defy,
>   And more than conquer all.'

So much for the first consequence Paul draws. Turn to the second. 'If Christ be not risen, *ye are yet in your sins.*' All the talk about being forgiven — pure delusion. All the noble words about God putting sins behind His back, or drowning them in the depths of the sea, or making the crimsoned page white as snow again — all mere mockery. Ye are yet in your sins, gripped, prisoned, slaves for life.

Now why? Why is that involved in it? Ah, you can see why. Because — if the Cross was the end — Christ's brave, pathetic attempt to be a Saviour failed. Because the sins of men that slew Him had the last word. Because Jesus, seeing the drift of this hateful thing across the pages, carrying its poisonous miasma with it, flung in His own body to try to break and stem and arrest the drift; but He did not break it — He was broken by it, and it rolled on over His dead body unheeding. So that there is no escape from the clutching hand of the past, no deliverance from the downward drag of our own souls. Ye are yet in your sins.

Well, does it matter? For us? 'The modern man,' said Sir Oliver Lodge, 'is not worrying about his sins, still less about their forgiveness.' 'Forgiveness?' cries Bernard Shaw, sweeping the whole thing aside as a cowardly flight from reality, 'forgiveness? That is a beggar's refuge! We must pay our debts.' Normally we do not trouble much about sin and forgiveness — morbid fictions, perhaps we think them. But I know this — once see what is really at stake here, once see that if forgiveness goes, then peace goes, and freedom goes, and happiness goes, and heaven goes — once see that, and you will cry with the very passion of despair, 'You shan't take that way! You shan't! You shan't!'

It does matter. You cannot live without it. There is a dreadful passage in Carlyle where he imagines a man trying to run away from his own shadow; and ever and again he turns round, and it is still there, that black thing, dogging him; on and on, flinging himself wildly away from it — and round again, and it is still there; and he is panting now, and dead-beat: 'God, God, I can't get away from it! I can't!' That is sin — if there is no forgiveness. Continually a man is left wondering — 'That old, unhappy deed — when will it spring on me? Where will it strike, and how?' King Herod slew John the Baptist in prison, and one day, months later, he heard about Jesus, and suddenly he trembled. 'This must be John back again,' he said, 'the man I killed, back from the dead!' It does matter, the thing called forgiveness. It matters so much that you can't live without it. And if Christ be not raised, it is gone.

But if Christ be risen from the dead — then sin is defeated! It has met its match. It is broken, blotted out, and you are free! You are like Christian, when the great burden he had carried on his bowed back to the cross, fell off there, and rolled and tumbled down the hill, gathering speed as it went, until it disappeared into the empty tomb of Christ and was never seen again; and the man stood there, stretching out his arms for the first time in his life in conscious and exultant freedom. All that — if Christ be raised. All that — for the spirits in prison. 'Yes,' cried Francis Thompson,

> 'God's mercy, I do think it well,
> Is flashed back from the brazen gates of Hell.'

Blessed be His name — 'delivered for our offences, raised again for our justification!'

So much for the second consequence Paul draws. Turn to the last. 'If Christ be not risen, *then they also which are fallen asleep in Christ are perished.*' Those whom we are accustomed to call 'the blessed departed' — obliterated, annihilated. Blown out of existence, as you would blow a candle out. 'Cast,' said Tennyson, 'as rubbish to the void.' Never to be met again. Perished.

Now why? Why is that involved in it? You can see why. You scarce need to ask. For if Jesus never rose, how should they? If the one finally perfect life that has ever appeared on earth did not get through this thing called Death — how should anyone else? They are perished.

Well, does it matter? Ah, don't say that! Don't mock us. Does anything else matter? As long as love is love, as long as one human heart cleaves and clings to another, it matters all the world!

You can't live without it. There was an old Welsh saint of a former generation, a great soldier of Christ — Christmas Evans they called him — and when the day came for him to die, he bade his friends at the bedside farewell, and turned his face to the wall; and in a little while, suddenly they saw him wave his hand triumphantly: 'Drive on! Drive on!' he cried, as if he were seeing Christ's chariots come to take him, 'Drive on!' And so he died. What if that were just delusion, and there were no chariots there? 'The angels!' cried a young boyish Covenanter on the scaffold in the grassmarket, just before the axe of death descended, 'the angels! They've come to carry me to Jesus' bosom!' And so he passed out. But what if that last cry were mistaken? What if Macbeth were right?

'Tomorrow, and tomorrow, and tomorrow,
Creeps in this petty pace from day to day,
To the last syllable of recorded time;
And all our yesterdays have lighted fools
The way to dusty death. Out, out brief candle!'

What if the Venerable Bede's image of our human life were all that could be said about it — a bird flying out of the dark into a brilliantly lighted banqueting-hall, flying across that brilliance for a moment, then out at the other window, out into the night again? Then we can only tell God that it is cruel of Him to put such love in our hearts, and snap it in the end! There is a picture by a great artist which shows God in the act of making His world. And as the vision of human life, with all its tragedy and loss, begins to shape itself out of chaos, a figure is seen starting up and crying to the Creator, 'God, if it is a world like that you are going to make, stay your hand! Don't make it at all!' That is how we should feel if death finishes love and destroys forever. And if Christ is not raised, it does.

But if Christ be risen from the dead — then they that have fallen asleep in Christ are alive, are ours, are here! 'Is there no one,' said Cromwell, as he lay dying and looked round on the faces of his weeping friends, 'is there no one here who will *praise the Lord*?' That is the new note. Grim, portentous, solemn Death — you thought you would rob me, did you? You were wrong.

'O thou soul of my soul! I shall clasp thee again,
   And with God be the rest!'

So Paul here has looked the grim thought — Christ not
risen — in the face, and challengingly has drawn the three
inevitable conclusions — faith gone, forgiveness gone,
immortality gone. But then, while the shudder of it is passing
over his readers' souls, comes his sudden burst of triumph.
'But now,' he cries, and every word of it is a trumpet-note,
a shout, a battle-cry — 'but now is Christ risen from the
dead' — and with that he sweeps the horror from his soul.
'Now is Christ risen!'

And if you ask him, 'How do you know it, Paul?' he
has two answers. 'Know it? Why, I have spoken with men
who have seen Him! Peter, Andrew, and John, and a
hundred others, men who have had their whole life changed
from top to bottom by the experience of seeing Him!' Can
you say that? Have you ever spoken to a man who had
seen the risen Christ? Some one surer of that than of anything else in life? That is one glorious line of evidence.

But Paul had another, an even greater. 'Christ risen —
how do I know it? I have seen Him myself, seen Him with
these very eyes, seen Him with this very heart!' And if anyone had dared to suggest to Paul that Christ was not really
alive — 'Not alive, man?' he would have answered, 'Why,
He arrested me riding to Damascus, and He has been power
to my life ever since! I have seen Him, felt Him — and I
know.' Can you say that? Say it in all sincerity, and with
no exaggeration at all — 'It is not I who live, but Christ
who lives in me: and I have actually felt His presence and
His power'? Then you have the evidence in yourself. You
know. And you can say, with Savonarola, 'They may kill me
if they please; but they will never, never, never tear the living
Christ from my heart!'

XVIII

A Modern Substitute for the Gospel

'Are not Abana and Pharpar, rivers of Damascus, better than all the waters of Israel? may I not wash in them, and be clean?' — 2 KINGS v. 12.

STEVENSON, IN A CHARMING LETTER DATED SEPTEMBER 1873, has described a day's walk in Fife, during which he came upon a labourer cleaning a byre, and fell into conversation. 'The man was to all appearance as heavy as any English clodhopper; but I knew I was in Scotland, and launched out forthright into Education and Politics and the aims of one's life.' As they talked together of this and that, one simple but memorable remark betrayed the real man — 'Him that has aye something ayont need never be weary.' 'And that,' comments Stevenson, 'from a man cleaning a byre!'

It is the apprehension of 'something beyond' which is the root of all religion. To define religion is, indeed, a well-nigh hopeless task: an American psychologist has collected no fewer than forty-eight proposed definitions, none of them, it is to be feared, entirely satisfactory. But if it is hard to find an adequate definition, we can at last point to one element linking all the religions of the world together, one common irreducible factor in which the very essence of religion appears to reside: the conviction, namely, of the reality of a world unseen, the sense that behind and beyond and above the material environment that we can touch and handle and control there lies something more, something which calls and signals to what is best within us, as deep calls to deep — in short, as Robert Browning put it,

> 'The feeling that there's God, He reigns and rules
> Out of this low world.'

A new spiritual horizon, a vital and liberating sense of a divine, directing power, communion with the eternal God — such is religion's offer. I wonder — how do we ourselves stand with regard to it? Have you found that horizon, that wonderful communion? Or would you have to confess unhappily, 'If that is religion, I am still outside: no such experience has ever come my way'?

Life presents us with two fundamental facts — man's search for God, God's search for man. But the strange, disquieting thing is that, though each is searching for the other, so often they fail to meet.

There must be some here today for whom this is a very personal problem. Indeed, I rather think that at times it has been the problem of us all; for there are moods in which religious feelings refuse to come, and days when spiritual perception has ebbed quite away.

Do you know the kind of experience I mean? You say your prayers, but it is like talking into the air: you have no vivid sense of any God who is listening. Perhaps after a while you stop praying altogether. What is the use of persevering, you say, when the whole thing has grown unreal? In church, it is somehow easier; though even there you have the feeling that the words of many of the hymns you are asked to sing breathe an assurance and a certainty which you would never claim to have reached, and that many of the Scripture passages seem to be dealing with emotions, raptures, and discoveries quite beyond your ken. It is the ever-old, ever-new problem: 'O that I knew where I might find Him!'

It brings a host of questions in its train. Is He a God to whom it is worth my while trying to pray? Is He a God who knows anything about it when things in my little corner of the universe get tangled and go wrong, and my heart is hurt and sore? Is He a God who can lay any hand of healing peace upon my soul when I am rushed and tired and growing hectic? Is He a God who has anything to say to a man left walking in the dark, when some of the kindly lights of life have gone out? Above all, is He a God who can help me when I have done something for which I hate myself? Has He any understanding and compassion and forgiveness and renewal for one who is feeling wretched and miserable and ashamed? O that I knew!

Here are some sentences from Hugh Walpole's story *Vanessa*. They are from the passage where Benjie, that misguided but strangely lovable character, is talking about Vanessa to his mother Elizabeth. ' "Vanessa is so good and so fine. She believes in God, you know, Mother." "And don't you?" "You know that I don't. Not as she does. Not as she does. I may be wrong. I dare say I am. But I *must* be honest. I don't *see* things that way. I'm ignorant. I don't know any more than the next fellow and I want the next fellow to believe as he sees, but I must be allowed to see for myself. I can't *see* God anywhere. The things that people believe are fine for them but nonsense to me. To me as I am now. I've got all my life in front of me and everything to learn. God may be proved to me yet. I hope He will be." "Proved!" Elizabeth laid her cheek for a moment against his. "God can't be proved, Benjie. He must be felt." "Yes, I suppose so. That may come to me one day. Meanwhile — a heathen and a vagabond can't marry Vanessa." ' '

'I can't *see* God anywhere. I can't realise Him in personal experience'. That, for countless thousands today, is the great crucial problem of religion and life. Indeed, many in our generation are feeling the problem so acutely that they are

almost prepared to drop the religion of their fathers altogether and to look out for some alternative.

Undoubtedly, the Great War, and even more, the heaped-
up disillusionments of the post-war years, have contributed
to this result. Take a book like Vera Brittain's *Testament of
Youth*, one of the most significant and revealing documents
of our times. Some of you may remember how she tells that
one of her earliest childhood memories concerned the
accession of King Edward VII to the throne, and the post-
ponement of the coronation owing to the King's sudden
illness. 'That night,' she says, 'I prayed earnestly to God to
make the dear King better and let him live. The fact that he
actually did recover established in me a touching faith in the
efficacy of prayer, which superstitiously survived until the
Great War proved to me, once for all, that there was nothing
in it.' That challenging sentence is typical of the revolt in
religion. Creeds and dogmas are abandoned. Beliefs once
regarded as fixed and settled have had their foundations
shaken. Even God, the sovereign Ruler of the universe,
is negated and dethroned. And many are on the look-out
now for some alternative to religous faith, some substitute
for the gospel of Christ.

Now the point to notice is this. That alternative is ready
to hand. A new religion has appeared on the field. A substitute for the gospel is offering itself. It is the worship, not of
God, but of man. This is the most serious rival which
Christianity in this generation is facing.

It is usually called humanism. But the name matters
little: it is the thing — the attitude of mind, the way of life —
with which we are concerned. Historically, of course, there
have been many brands of humanism. Thus, for example,
you have the humanism of Protagoras and the Greek sophists,
five centuries before Christ, with their significant watchword, 'Man is the measure of all things'. At the other end of

the scale, superficially similar, yet ethically of quite different lineage, there is the humanism of Swinburne, with his cheap sneer at Jesus, the 'pale Galilean', and his 'Glory to man in the highest, for man is the master of things!' There is the optimistic humanism of Herbert Spencer and the Victorians, sadly shaken, it must be confessed, by the trend of recent events; and there is the pessimistic humanism of Bertrand Russell, who pictures the individual soul left to 'struggle alone against the whole weight of a universe that cares nothing for its hopes and fears'. There is the scientific humanism of Julian Huxley's 'religion without revelation', and there is the hedonistic humanism of Aldous Huxley's 'brave new world'.

But, broadly speaking, what confronts us today as the declared rival of the Christian faith is the theory that puts man in the centre of the picture; that summons him — the old accepted standards of ethics having been eaten away by what Lippmann has called 'the acids of modernity' — to work out his own salvation and construct his own scheme of values; that pins its faith to science and education and mechanism and human brains for the redeeming of the world, rather than to grace and the divine initiative; that seeks, with the aid of psychology, to explain away the supernatural element in religion, reducing Christian belief to mere 'phantasy-thinking' or 'projection'; that substitutes self-expression for Christ's demand of self-surrender, the dictatorship of instinct for the rule of God, and culture for the cross.

Let us, however, give this rival creed its due. There are scores of thousands of people today — especially young men and women — for whom organised religion has lost its grip; and when these sincerely seeking for something that may fill up what H. G. Wells has called 'the God-shaped blank in their heart', turn to one or another of the different substitutes for religion now offering themselves, it is doing the cause of Christ no service simply to denounce their revolt. Sympathy and an understanding heart — these we require: not the negative censoriousness which effects nothing, and is in any case terribly unlike Jesus. Admittedly, what we are witnessing is a revolt; but when you have called it that, you have not necessarily discredited it. For, as Canon F. R. Barry has incisively reminded us, 'Mrs Grundy, when all is said and done, was not a pattern of Christian conduct.' Nor can anyone seriously deny that between the mind of Christ on the one hand, and conventional Christian ethics on the other, there has sometimes been a deep divergence: witness the toleration too often in the past extended by the ethical standards of the time to such things as wars of aggression, and slums, and desperate inequalities, and villainous social conditions. In so far as the champions of the revolt have stood for the dignity for personality and for the opportunity of fullness of life for all men, their influence has been salutary; and any Christianity that is not prepared to work this demand out in practice is less than fully Christian.

Nor should it be forgotten that the movement of revolt, at its best, has been a challenge to religion to rescue for the praise and service of God those glories of art and beauty which the Church, at one stage of its career, seemed willing to assign indiscriminately to the world, the flesh, and the devil; and that, again through its best representatives, it has been a constant reminder that it is our duty to keep religion free from the obscurantist spirit which is fundamentally irreligious, to welcome new knowledge eagerly, and fearlessly to follow wherever truth may lead. In these ways, the rival creed — at its best — has made a real contribution to the onward march of mankind; and of some at least of those who have professed it, God's word Cyrus might be spoken — 'I girded thee, though thou hast not known Me.'

The trouble about the modern worship of humanity is that it is *too* human. It cannot see beyond man. It clings pathetically to the exploded myth of mankind's self-re-deemability. It has an uneasy feeling that somewhere at the heart of its own chosen religion there lurks a radical fallacy. It begins to suspect that its idol has feet of clay. And thus between thoroughgoing scientific naturalism on the one hand, and whole-hearted Christian faith on the other, it stands swithering and undecided, maintaining a precarious equilibrium. It has nothing more satisfying to offer the hungry world than the religion of 'disinterestedness, detach-ment, and maturity of character', which Lippmann so eloquently preaches: 'Stoicism in plus-fours', as Canon Barry perhaps rather irreverently calls it. But this is simply to offer a stone to those who are clamouring for bread. It is to misunderstand completely the real problem mankind is facing. Naaman might extol his Abana and Pharpar: but the one question which mattered was, 'Could they make a leper clean?' And our modern vaunted Abanas and Pharpars — the disinterestedness and the culture and the scientific spirit of the age — have undoubtedly much to contribute to the welfare of the race. But that is not the question. The question is, Have they cleansing and regenerating power? The predominantly pessimistic tone which characterises so much of the modern literature of humanism is an implicit confession of defeat. Even H. G. Wells has his 'anatomy of frustration' now. Something else is needed. A power that is more than human must come into action. *Go, wash in Jordan.*

The rock on which our modern substitutes for the gospel go to pieces is the basic act of sin. Lippmann himself, at the outset of his *Preface to Morals*, makes the significant confes-sion: 'We have come to see that Huxley was right when he said that "a man's worst difficulties begin when he is able to do as he likes". The evidences of these greater difficulties lie all about us.' And in this age when a great word like 'Puritanism' is so often merely a gibe; when scores of voices are perpetrating the fallacy that man can have, and ought to have, absolute, unbridled freedom to do as he likes, and to drive his way down any path of self-expression that he chooses; when so many others (taking their cue from that) begin to believe that almost anything can be justified in the sacred name of the new morality — and proceed to talk in a silly self-conscious way (thinking themselves the champions of emancipation) about things which are supposed to be clever, but which are not clever in the least, which are indeed just common sins, and rotten, selfish sins at that — in this age we need to have it written upon our minds, as with a pen of iron on the rock, that God's will, God's truth, God's throne, God's everlasting decisive difference between right and wrong, that difference for which Christ died, stand as fast and as binding as ever, and claim every decent soul's allegiance.

To endeavour to explain sin away — as 'humanity's growing pains', or 'good in the making', or 'the stock-in-trade of a morbid theology' — is simply flippant. If the desperate sickness of the world at this moment is not sufficient rebuke to that superficiality, there remains the inward witness of the individual heart, refusing to consent to any such cheap self-deception. No doubt, for many today, the noise of the machine and the jangle of the wheels of progress have drowned the words of the ancient cry, 'O wretched man that I am! Who shall deliver me?' But that cry, for all who have ears to hear, still breaks from baffled hearts the world over; and every movement that claims to speak to this generation must stand and be tested here. For no man can fulfil his true nature until sin's twist and bias have been met and dealt with — that is to say, until his personality has been transformed, or, as Jesus put it, 'born from above', 'redeemed'. No man can stand up free until a power that is greater than his own has entered into him. It takes the supernatural to burst the chains of the natural. Man must have God.

Do you see now why our modern substitutes for the gospel are so finally unsatisfying? Behind their ethical bankruptcy and powerlessness lies their scepticism about the unseen and the eternal. This is the fundamental irrationality. Eliminate the supernatural, we are being told today, if you would be a realist. How often that singularly inept and muddled argument is reiterated! The fact of the matter is that it is precisely the man who believes in the supernatural with all his being (using that word, not in its popular and mistaken sense of 'contra-natural', but as referring to an order above the natural, prior to it, controlling it and holding it together), it is he who is the only true realist. He is actually more scientific, if you care to put it so, than his sceptic brother. For he knows better than to allow the visible and the tangible and the material to obsess and tyrannise him. He has seen deep enough into the heart of life to realise once for all that the real forces are the invisible ones. You can't see personality. Yet what a force personality is. You can't see love. But let love get hold of a man, and it can transform him utterly. You can't see life. Yet life is the most creative thing in the universe. And as the invisible things — personality and love and life and beauty and truth and goodness — are all summed up in God, the religious faith which lives, moves, and has its being in God is the true and final realism.

The task of the church, faced by the modern challenge, is surely abundantly clear. It is to proclaim a full evangel, in all its width and sweep and power and splendour. It is to cease arguing the case for religion, and to concentrate instead on heralding the living God. It is to refuse to be deflected by one degree from its primary commission, which is to hold up Christ, crucified, risen, exalted. We hear a great deal to-day about the difficulties with which organised religion in this generation has to contend. Difficulties indeed there are; but let that not obscure the fact that, for a Church possessing the passion of evangelism, this is an hour of quite unexampled opportunity. For tens of thousands, disillusioned by the failure of all the alternatives for Christ, are now ready to hear of some more excellent way; and it is as true today as when the words were first spoken long ago — 'I, if I be lifted up from the earth, will draw all men unto Me.'

XIX

Our Duty of Praise

'Praise ye the Lord. Praise the Lord, O my soul. While
I live will I praise the Lord: I will sing praises unto my
God while I have any being.' — Ps. cxlvi. 1, 2.

ALL THE WAY THROUGH THE BOOK OF PSALMS, EVEN IN ITS
most sorrow-laden passages, you feel that you are walking
on a smouldering volcano of praise, liable to burst out at
any moment into a great flame of gratitude to God. And as
the book draws to its close, the flame leaps clear from the
smoke: here you have praise, and nothing but praise.

You have perhaps watched a great conductor bringing
every member of his orchestra into action towards the close
of some mighty music, have seen him, as the music climbed
higher and higher, signalling to one player after another,
and always at the signal another instrument responding to
the summons and adding its voice to the music, until at the
last crashing chords not one was left dumb, but all were
uniting in a thrilling and triumphant climax. So these final
psalms summon everything in creation to swell the glorious
unison of God's praise. They signal to the sun riding in the
heavens, 'You come in now, and praise Him!' — then to the
myriad stars of night, 'You now, praise Him!' — then to
the mountains, raking the clouds with their summits, 'Praise
Him!' — then to the kings and judges of the earth, 'Praise
Him!' — then to young manhood in its strength and
maidenhood in its grace and beauty, 'Praise Him!' — then
to the multitude of saints in earth and heaven, 'Praise Him!'
— until the wide universe is shouting with every voice the

praise of God alone. 'While I live,' cries the psalmist, 'will I praise the Lord: I will sing praises unto my God while I have any being.'

Now that is religion. That is the test of religion. Wherever you have real religion, be sure of this — the dominant note will be praise. That is why, when you come down the centuries to Christianity, you find that there is more praise in it than in all the other religions of the world put together.

Some religions there are which are not strong in praise. They have very little if any song about them at all. Mohammedanism, for example. Mohammedanism knows how to wield the scimitar: it does not know how to strike the harp. Or Stoicism. The Stoic creed is great and noble and rugged in endurance: but it is poor and dry and barren in song. Or Puritanism of a certain stamp — not the splendid, positive Puritanism of Milton, Cromwell, and Bunyan, but the negative, reactionary, repressive Puritanism of which Edmund Gosse, for instance, gave such a memorable picture in *Father and Son* — that is religion without a note of praise about it. But what makes Christianity, what differentiates Christianity, is the sounding out all the way through it — even in the tears and anguish of it — of the one diapason note, praise to God. 'While I live', says this man, and we who have seen Christ, and who know something at least of the difference Christ can make, ought to say it even more emphatically than he, 'while I live will I praise the Lord: I will sing praises unto my God while I have any being'.

That is our function as Christians, our first duty and our last. Are we fulfilling it? Take it of our prayers. Is praise always the keynote there? Or are our prayers not sometimes a kind of aggrieved and querulous protest to a God who seems to manage things so badly for us? One or two of the earlier psalmists are like that when they are on their knees, saying in effect 'Now, God, just look at your universe —

look at my own unhappy miserable lot! Is this all you can do for me, O God?' — and so on through verse after verse of lugubrious, ungrateful self-pity; though indeed if you read these same psalms right through you nearly always come to a point where the man pulls himself up, as though in a kind of sudden access of shame that makes him blush, and then (as St. Paul would say) in 'indignation and revenge' at himself, sweeps the low mood from his soul; and before he is finished he is crying — 'Praise God from whom all blessings flow!' Never let us forget that praise is to be the keynote, the beginning, middle, and end, of every prayer.

Or take it of our hymns and songs. Is praise the keynote there? Ah, sometimes to hear us Christians sing, you would hardly guess (certainly a stranger coming amongst us would never guess) that it is the most glorious theme in the world we are celebrating! Take some of the great Easter hymns, for instance — songs like 'Jesus Christ is risen today', or 'The strife is o'er, the battle done'. I cannot understand anyone who does not want to stand up and sing these with all his heart and mind, to stand with soul on tiptoe, as it were, and with every fibre of his spiritual being in it — which is the only right way to sing when it is the risen Christ of whom you are singing. Or take a hymn like 'For all the saints', mounting up at last to that mighty verse:

'But, lo! there breaks a yet more glorious day;
    The saints triumphant rise in bright array;
    The King of Glory passes on His way.
        Hallelujah!'

Quite frankly, I cannot understand anyone who, when that is being sung, does not lift up his head and put his very self into it, not with any mumbled, self-conscious, uncertain Hallelujah at the end, which may mean anything or nothing, but with a real, ringing, confident 'Hallelujah!' Gairdner of

Cairo one day, speaking of the 'Hallelujah Chorus', exclaimed, 'What an opportunity for a sanctified shout to God!' That was putting it crudely no doubt, but the root of the matter was there. The very foundations of the empire of darkness, declares one of the marching-songs of the Church, 'quiver at the shout of praise'. Do they, indeed? Do our Christian songs really make the principalities and powers of that dim empire tremble to hear them, as the Cavaliers trembled when Cromwell's Ironsides raised their psalms? Are we realising that praise is the central act of worship — not something to be drifted through indifferently, and so on to something more important — but actually the central thing? For that is the truth. And we have all to take our share and make it central — this duty of praise to God.

But even that is only touching the surface of the matter yet. For after all, it is not just a question of our prayers and hymns: it is a question of the whole tone of our life. Is praise the keynote there? Some people indeed there are who are constitutionally low-set, always more conscious of the clouds than of the blue skies of life. Nearly everyone passes through phases of that. Even Martin Luther, brave, high-spirited soul as he was, burst out one day — 'The world's an evil fellow; let's hope God will soon end him!' We do experience these low moods when the fountains of praise and gratitude in us are all dried up. 'The world's winter is going,' said George Eliot on such a day, 'but my everlasting winter is setting in.'

The question is, How are we to avoid that, and keep a perpetually praising spirit? Well, it is partly at least a matter of right selection. I mean that when praise and gratitude wither and decay, it is because we have been concentrating on the wrong things. If a man fixes on his disadvantages and difficulties, and gazes all the time at these, it is the easiest thing in the world to get up a case against God. It is almost inevitable that he develops the Omar Khayyàm attitude, the 'sorry scheme of things' attitude, which wants to shatter the whole plan to bits and start anew.

Hence the praising, grateful spirit is, partly at least, a matter of right selection. No man ought to start totalling up his disadvantages till he has sat down first to count his mercies. When you experience the pull of the low mood, and feel that there is a host of things against you, and that your lot is surely harder than most, then is the time to cry to your own soul, 'Halt! All that may be true enough, all these hard things may be there, but before we look at that, soul of mine, you and I are going to do something else: we are going to look at the providences!' It is a Christian's duty to fix on the mercies first. And they are always there. 'You call the chess-board black,' says Browning's Bishop Blougram in effect, 'but try looking at it from another point, and see if you don't have to call it white!' A friend in trouble once wrote to Charles Lamb that the world seemed 'drained of all its sweets'. To which Lamb replied, 'Drained of its sweets? I don't know what you mean. Are there not roses and violets still in the earth, and the sun and moon still reigning in heaven?' The man was not looking for the providences. Borrow's gipsy knew better. 'In blindness,' said he, 'there's still the wind on the heath!' Once when Rainy, the great churchman, was passing through a time of public obloquy and misunderstanding, a sympathetic friend said to him that he did not know how Rainy could bear it. 'Ah, but then, you see,' came the quiet answer with a smile, 'I'm very happy at home!' Yes, the darkest night has stars in it, and a Christian is a man who fixes not on the darkness but on the stars; and especially on the one bright and morning star that is always shining — Jesus! When the low mood comes, open your New Testament. Read it imaginatively. Stand on the shore at Capernaum. Visit the home at Bethany. Sit by Jacob's well, and in the upper room. Look into

Jesus' eyes. Listen to His voice. Take a walk round by Calvary. Remember the crown of thorns. Then tell yourself (for it is true), 'All this was for me! The Son of God loved me, and gave Himself for me.' And see if a passion of praise does not send the low mood flying, and you begin to feel like Charles Kingsley when he wrote to a friend, 'Must we not thank, and thank, and thank for ever, and toil and toil for ever for Him?' 'While I live I will praise Thee: I will sing praises to my God while I have any being.'

But this question of making a right selection is not the inmost secret yet. We may train ourselves to praise by fixing on our mercies rather than on our disadvantages. But the whole lesson has not been learnt till we can praise God for everything, the clouds as well as the sunshine, the darkness as well as the stars.

Now this I believe to be the supreme value to us of the men who wrote the psalms. They stand, these men at every turn of the road, facing every sort of experience that can come to us, and there they cry, 'Praise ye the Lord!' They stand over our sick-beds and say, 'Praise ye the Lord!' They stand beside our worst disappointments and cry, 'Praise ye the Lord!' They stand beside our open graves and whisper, 'Praise ye the Lord!' That is faith's victory.

There is one tremendous page of Scripture on which we are shown a saint of God visited by trouble, one terrible blow after another coming down on him until his whole life was reeling; and when the bitter day that had beggared and ruined him was closing, Job, with set face and clenched hands and bent head, was sitting there, muttering something almost fiercely and desperately to himself: 'The Lord gave, the Lord hath taken away.' And to begin with, I imagine, he could not get beyond that, could not add another word, but only kept on repeating it in a stunned dazed, uncertain way, 'The Lord gave, and the Lord hath taken.' And then there was dead silence. And for a moment everything was in the balance, his soul, his religion, his attitude to God, his very life, everything in the balance; and in the silence it was just as if the unseen world and all God's guardian angels were waiting for what would come next, wondering if it would be the soul's last cry of desolation, some dreadful anathema on life and God and heaven — waiting, wondering while he fought his battle out; but then suddenly, breaking the silence, half a sob and half a shout it came, 'Blessed be the name of the Lord!' Faith's victory! Praise from the depths!

Old Alan Cameron, the Covenanter, was lying a prisoner in the Tolbooth in Edinburgh, when suddenly the door of his cell burst open and in came soldiers, carrying something. 'Look!' they said, uncovering it. And Alan Cameron looked. It was the head of his own boy Richard, slain for Christ. And the old man staggered as if struck in the face with a whip. But then he lifted his head. 'It is the Lord,' he said, 'good is the will of the Lord.' Faith's victory!

Ah, now we know what the prophet meant who called not only on the flowers and trees to sing their pæan to the God of hosts, but on the bare desolate ruins and dead ashes of a glory that had been humbled to the dust: 'Sing together, ye waste places of Jerusalem!' For the last victory of the saints is to be able to praise God for everything — even as Jesus took the bread in token of His body and broke it, and over that broken symbol gave God thanks; took the cup, brimming over with all the bitterness of death, and gave God thanks; went out from the upper room to Gethsemane's sweat and agony, singing a hymn, and giving God thanks! It is that grateful, praising Christ who can make us sons of praise like Himself, men and women who have found the secret of a fortitude stronger than any pain, of a peace unshaken by any assaults of doubt, and of a joy that smiles through the blinding tears of defeated dreams and the bitterest disappointments that human hearts can know. It is only Jesus who can guarantee the soul's high victory. But His power to do it is unquestioned. He can make us strong, in face of everything, to praise the Lord, and to sing praises unto our God while we have any being.

So we come back finally to this, that Christian praise is not in any sense a mere matter of inclination: it is a matter of simple duty. And it is a duty in three directions.

It is our duty to God. There was a day when Jesus on the road healed ten lepers; and one of them, finding that that living death was really over, came running back to pour his grateful soul at Jesus' feet. 'Where are the other nine?' asked Jesus. And he must be deaf indeed who does not hear in that question something like the hurt sob of the Son of God.

> 'Blow, blow, thou winter wind,
> Thou art not so unkind
> As man's ingratitude'

to God! 'Where are the nine?'

Isaiah, in a day of national apostasy, when all God's toil in His chosen vineyard seemed ending in nothing but a harvest of rank weeds, heard God crying, 'What more could have been done in My vineyard than what I have done?' After all that — this! The Galilean pilgrims and all the friends of Jesus were shouting their Hosannas round Him as He rode into Jerusalem on the first Palm Sunday long ago, when some sour-faced people approached and advised Him to rebuke them. 'I tell you,' retorted Christ, 'if these should hold their peace, the very stones would cry out!' And must we not say that if, after what God in Christ has done for us, delivering our eyes from tears and our feet from falling and our souls from death, if after that we are not simply throbbing with gratitude and praise, then the stones of the street

T–G

and the stones of the houses where we live, and the stones of the church where we worship, might well cry out against us? Praise is our duty to God.

It is our duty to our own souls. In the story of that saintly soul who died some years ago, Francis Chavasse, Bishop of Liverpool, one favourite sentence of the Bishop's stands out as a guiding light of all his life — 'Praise and service are great healers.' It is worth trying to get inside the meaning of that. Praise and service are great healers. In other words, when life grows sore and wounding, and it is difficult to be brave, praise God; and if it is hard to do it, make yourself do it, and in the very act of praise the wound will begin to heal. Sing something, and you will rally your own heart with the song! Praise and service are great healers. Praise brings the wounded back to life's firing-line again. And thus praise is our duty to our own souls.

It is our duty to our brother man. For Christian praise has this property about it — that it is contagious. One song begets another, and the spark of praise leaps from heart to heart. One man with praise to God in his soul will start others singing who would never have thought of raising the song themselves. It is said of that great missionary-soldier of Jesus, Francis Xavier, by one of his own contemporaries, that if ever any of the brothers were sad, the way they took to be happy was just to go and look at him. That is how your praise can help. It is a troubled, tangled world in which we are living now; and God knows there is enough darkness in it without our doing anything, by dullness or depression or sullen cynicism, to make that darkness deeper. The real servant of humanity today is the man whose life breathes praise. Keep sounding that note, and even when you do not know it, others will be facing life more valiantly because of you, and it may be thanking God that ever you were born.

XX

O Come, O Come, Immanuel!

'Comfort ye, comfort ye my people, saith your God. Speak ye comfortably to Jerusalem, and cry unto her, that her warfare is accomplished, that her iniquity is pardoned.' — ISAIAH xl. 1, 2.

TODAY WE ARE STANDING IN THE GATEWAY OF THE ADVENT season; and I wish that the authentic thrill of Advent could lay some deep spell upon our spirits.

What does Advent mean? It means the glory of the coming of the Lord. It means the breaking in of the divine into human history, of the supernatural into the natural. It means a sense of something great impending from the side of heaven.

The world is blundering in a morass of sin and sorrow now, and Abyssinia goes out into the dark, and the streets of Spain run blood, and men lose hope completely; but here and there some man, some group of men, some Church stands listening and intent — for God is marching on. That is Advent.

And people have their personal problems too: and there are brave faces which hide sore hearts, and secret wounds that ache, and a restlessness new every morning; and life is terribly much harder for some than any who see them can imagine, and even God seems to have forgotten to be gracious; but sometimes through the darkness shines a light, and the troubled heart grows calm again. 'Be still, my soul; for God will surely come.' That is Advent.

I wish we could all recapture the authentic thrill of this

dear Advent time. But words are poor things to convey it:
it needs the wings of music. Some of us were listening to
Sir Walford Davies's recent broadcast talk on 'Melodies of
Christendom'. 'We want to help you to catch the Advent
spirit,' he said; and then his singers sang — sang first one of
those mighty melodies of Bach in which the passionate,
desperate yearning of generations and centuries of men have
been caught and concentrated, sang next of the joy when
midnight turns to morning:

> " 'Wake, awake! for the night is flying,'
> The watchmen on the heights are crying,
> 'Awake, Jerusalem, at last!' "

I think that songs and hymns and music can carry us nearer
to the burning heart of the Advent message than all the
sermons and discourses in the world. And so I hope that
what I cannot do may be accomplished for some in this
church today when the time comes for us to sing our final
hymn, that great cry of the souls of men which the Church
for eight hundred years has lifted up to heaven: 'O come, O
come, Immanuel' (you cannot sing it without seeing a
multitude of hands stretched out to God in passionate
pleading down the ages):

> 'O come, O come, Immanuel,
> And ransom captive Israel,
> That mourns in lonely exile here
> Until the Son of God appear' —

and then — the great crashing chords of triumphant re-
assurance:

> 'Rejoice! rejoice! Immanuel
> Shall come to thee, O Israel.'

That is Advent.

And that is the spirit of our text. 'Comfort ye, comfort ye My people, saith your God.' I know, of course, that the Advent gospel has another side to it. I know there is a day of the Lord that is like a thief in the night. I have read the Word of God, and heard its great commission — 'Cry aloud! Spare not! Lift up thy voice like a trumpet!' I have heard the terrible, startling urgency that was in the voice of Jesus when He tried to shake men awake from their sleep, lest they should be found with loins ungirt and lamps unlit when at midnight came the cry. But I know also this, that beneath all the drums and thunder of the Advent Symphony there is a deeper undertone, the music of the peace of God that passeth understanding. 'Comfort ye, comfort ye My people, saith your God.'

'If I had my ministry to live through again,' said a dear saint of God at the close of a long life, 'I should strike the note of comfort far oftener than I have done.' I think one begins to understand that. And if there were only one more sermon to preach, one last message to deliver, before the night descended, and the kindly lights of life went out, I think the text would have to be, not 'Be not deceived, God is not mocked', nor anything of the kind, but rather this: 'The eternal God is thy refuge, and underneath are the everlasting arms', or those dearest of the words of Jesus, 'Come unto Me, all ye that labour and are heavy laden', or this of Jesus' greatest herald, 'Comfort ye, comfort ye My people, saith your God.'

This is not being sentimental. There is undoubtedly a type of character which accepts the consolations of religion, wallows in them in fact, without ever facing the challenge of religion. That is sentimental. That is the kind of follower who brings down the name of Jesus in the eyes of the world. 'Sentimentalism is enjoyment without obligation', said George Meredith. But the true comfort of Christ is a strong, bracing, reinforcing thing. It is like a wind to a boat that has been becalmed. It is like the gift of a job to a man who has been for years out of work. It is like the clasp of a friend's hand in time of need. This is certainly the root idea of the word 'comfort' in the New Testament; and when Jesus speaks of the Holy Spirit as the 'Comforter', He is really giving a promise that God will stand by a man in the day of his need, and brace his heart and nerve his arm, and make him more than conqueror. It ought surely to be possible to proclaim that without sentimentalism. I should be failing you if I attempted for one moment to minimise or to conceal the essential hardness of Christianity: it is going to be hard to the end of the day. But I should be failing you even more if I did not tell you of this comforting Christ. 'Speak ye comfortably to Jerusalem', or, as the words are better translated, 'Speak ye home to the heart of Jerusalem'; and 'Comfort ye My people, saith your God.'

Jerusalem! Think of her for a moment. How terribly she needed comfort! All that chequered history behind her — the dreams that flickered out on Mount Gilboa, where Saul and Jonathan lay dead ('Ye daughters of Israel, weep over Saul: how are the mighty fallen!'), the glory of David tarnished by the unguarded hour when Bathsheba meant more to him than God, the long battle of the prophets with recrudescent paganism when Baal renewed his hold, the thunder of Sennacherib's legions down the plains of Esdraelon and across the borders of Judah, the bitterness of the Babylonian bondage when the exiles wept for Zion and the harps hung silent on the willows ('How shall we sing the Lord's song in a strange land? If I forget thee, O Jerusalem!'), the eyes peering through the dark, the voices crying 'How long, O Lord, how long?' the hands battering importunately at heaven's gate, the cry from the last ramparts of the soul, 'Watchman! Watchman! Will the night soon pass?' All that

— for centuries — and then, 'Comfort ye, comfort ye My people, saith your God!' And so the new dawn came.

It was needed then, that note of comfort: is it not needed now? Think of God looking down at this world today, where man at war with man cannot hear the love-song of the angels, God seeing all the pathetic wreckage of broken hopes with which the sea of life is littered, and man's struggles and gropings for the light — what do you imagine God must be feeling, as He contemplates the human scene? Anger? Impatience? Contempt? Disdain? Surely the writer of the old psalm knew better when, out of his own experience of what life and parenthood had taught him, he wrote the words, 'Like as a father pitieth his children, so pitieth the Lord!'

You will remember a poem of Coventry Patmore's — 'The Toys', he calls it — which tells how one day his little son, having been disobedient, was sent to bed unkissed, and how the father, relenting, crept up later that night into the room, and there the child lay asleep, his face still wet with tears; and near his head on a little table he had gathered some of his favourite toys — a box of counters, a few shells, one or two copper coins — to comfort his sad small heart; and as the father kissed those childish tears away and left others of his own, it occurred to him that perhaps God might be feeling towards all His sons and daughters of this world just as he felt that night towards his own sleeping child:

> 'When Thou rememberest of what toys
> We made our joys,
> How weakly understood
> Thy great commanded good,
> Then, fatherly not less
> Than I whom Thou hast moulded from the clay
> Thou'lt leave Thy wrath, and say,
> "I will be sorry for their childishness." '

'Like as a father pitieth, so pitieth the Lord His children.'
And surely if ever that was true, it must be true about this
wayward, blundering, unhappy world today; and 'Comfort
ye My people, saith your God.'

But God does not deal with men in the mass, and to talk
about God comforting the world may sound remote and
leave us cold. It is the individual message of Advent we
want to capture. What does this deep saying in Isaiah mean
for me? There are souls by the ten thousand needing comfort
today. Has Advent anything for them?

I think, as one grows older, one learns to look at humanity
with new eyes of wonder and of reverence: for countless are
the hidden heroisms of every day. Doubtless a cynic, looking
at human nature, will see only drabness and mediocrity
and commonplaceness and irritating stupidity; but the
man who sees only that — though he be the cleverest wit
imaginable — is proclaiming himself blind and a fool. He is
missing everything. He is missing the shining gallantry and
fortitude which are everywhere in action. You cannot go
through this world with your eyes open, and with some
degree of sympathy in your soul, without realising sooner or
later that one of the crowning glories of the world — a thing
that might well make the morning stars sing together and the
sons of God shout for joy — is the sheer valour with which
multitudes of men and women, quite unknown to fame, are
carrying themselves in the face of difficulties calculated to
break their hearts.

Take any gathered company of people — think of the
troubled spirits that are there among them, baffled and bewildered because life has treated them unkindly, and yet
keeping their heads up, and making no complaint; some
worried about their health, wondering how long they will
be able to keep going, and what will happen to their dear
ones when they finally have to give in; men out in the world,

bearing the burden and heat of the day, and strained almost to the limit of their endurance by the fierce competition of of this modern age; fathers and mothers anxious about children whose characters seem subtly changing, losing something of the frankness and fineness and tenderness that once was there; young people grappling with temptations which they have never been able to tell to anyone; souls that have gone down defeated in the fight, despising themselves for their defeat, eager for some secret that will turn defeat to victory; lives that have had their hour of thrilling joy and springtime, and then it has vanished, and the world has grown grey and chill and wintry, and weary all life's journey now, on to the very end; conflicts which none can understand except the one who has to face them; lonelinesses that hurt; disabilities that handicap; renunciations that are a crown of thorns; memories that bless, and memories that burn, and memories that are a crucifixion. Ah, friends, look on any gathering of your fellow-men and women, try to see them, not with the eyes of cheap criticism, but with the eyes of God — and you will behold there the gold of courage, and the shining precious jewels of a chivalry like the chivalry of Christ.

More than that. You will wish to God that you could be a helper and a comforter. One feels so helpless often. It is like watching a loved one suffering some terrible physical pain. 'Oh God, why cannot I suffer this instead? Lord, give it to me, and let that other off!' One feels so helpless. And one so longs to help. Principal Denney was listening one day to a friend of his own, a missionary from the New Hebrides, telling the graphic story of how one of the New Hebridean islands had received the comfort of the gospel, and had been changed from darkness to light. And when the story was over, 'I'd rather had done a work like that,' said Denney, 'than have written all the best books in the library.' And there are hours — I am sure they must have come to you —

when you would rather have been able to comfort one dear soul in trouble than have known all the speculative philosophy in the world. 'Comfort ye, comfort ye My people, saith your God.'

Have you ever thought how utterly Jesus devoted Himself to this? There are commentators who tell us that Jesus did His miracles of healing to impress the onlookers and to prove His claims. I think not. He did them because He could not bear to see God's children suffering. The poor mother of Nain, crying as if her heart would break as she stumbled after the pathetic little procession going out to bury her only son — Christ could not bear it! The leper, the innocent, once gay young life struck down by that slow, dreadful living death — Christ could not bear it. 'I will: be thou clean.' The great mass of attractive, lovable men and women caught in the toils of sins that spoilt their lives, and temptations they could not break, and wild regrets that were a misery — Christ could not bear it. And so He died to free them. And so we can say today, in those most moving words, of our hymn, 'Jesus, Thou art all compassion' (I beg you never sing these words unthinkingly, but take them home to yourself, and say, 'This is true, and true for me.),

> 'Jesus, Thou art all compassion,
>   Pure, unbounded love Thou art;
> Visit us with Thy salvation
>   Enter every trembling heart.'

But the greatest thing of all is this, that when you see this compassionate Christ, you are seeing God. This is the comfort which the Advent tidings bring — and it is all in that one word Immanuel: for Immanuel means 'God with us', with us in Jesus, God going through the darkness with you, God saying, 'My friend, you must not carry the trouble alone any longer — cast it down at My feet: I will take it and carry it, and the hardest part shall be My part!' The word Immanuel means that where we, with all our poor human words of comfort, break down utterly, God begins. Immanuel means that when you feel nobody wants you, God does. Immanuel means that when your heart is crying to every would-be comforter, 'Ah, you don't undertand, you can't see things from my side of them, you are outside' — Immanuel means that God is right inside. Immanuel means God with you and in you, God making the pain a sacrament, the conflict a crusade, and the broken dreams a ladder up to heaven. And so, through Christ, God speaks home to the heart of Jerusalem.

But you know and I know that there is one comfort we need more than any other, more than the soothing of our sorrows and the calming of our cares; and that is, the forgiving of our sins. There is no real comfort until the conscience is at peace, and the heart is clean, and the will is right with God. But the glory of this great word Immanuel is that it means even that. For listen to what stands written. It is not only 'Speak to the heart of Jerusalem,' but 'cry unto her' that her iniquity is pardoned!' And it is 'Cry to her' this time, not 'Speak quietly to her heart,' but 'Cry it aloud!' — as much as to say, 'She will not believe it at first. She will not want to accept it. It will sound too good to be true. You will have to make this tidings urgent. Cry to her that all is forgiven!'

It is on that level that God's greatest work is done. I began by saying that I wished I could help you to capture the authentic thrill of Advent. I end now by saying that this is it — nothing less — that if on those battlefields where men and women struggle for their souls we have sometimes met defeat; if things have happened and have left a mark, and we know they ought never to have been; if the shades of the prison-house of habit have come closing in around us; if we have tasted shame, and self-despising, and have lost the

morning freshness of our souls; if, like those Jews in Babylon, we have felt ourselves exiled from the face of God —
then this is the thrill of Advent, to hear the great Father
saying, 'My son, My daughter, that is all past now, and done
with and finished forever,' to find every barrier broken
down by the love of Christ and the old dear intimacy res-
tored, to know that you can enter, this very moment, into a
new world of light and joy and liberty. We are going to sing
of it now, in the greatest of Advent songs. God grant the
experience of it to us all!

> 'O come, Thou Key of David come,
> And open wide our heavenly home;
> Make safe the way that leads on high,
> And close the path to misery.
>
> Rejoice! rejoice! Immanuel
> Shall come to thee, O Israel.'

XXI

Love's Last Appeal

'Having yet therefore one son, his well-beloved, he
sent him also last unto them, saying, They will reverence
my Son. But those husbandmen said among themselves,
This is the heir; come, let us kill him, and the inherit-
ance shall be ours. And they took him, and killed him,
and cast him out of the vineyard. What shall therefore
the lord of the vineyard do?' — MARK xii. 6–9.

TO READ THE PARABLES OF JESUS IN THE GOSPELS IS TO MOVE
through a wonderful picture-gallery, full of the most
fascinating portraits — the Good Samaritan, the Younger
Son, the Elder Brother, the Sower, the Shepherd, the Pearl
Merchant, and many more — all painted by the hand of the
great Master Artist. In one dim corner of the gallery, dim
because the sunlight which falls upon the other pictures is
here toned down and shadowed by a cross, hangs the Artist's
self-portrait. Will you stand there with me for a few moments
now, and let this picture speak to you?

For this parable, as Jesus told it, was sheer autobiography.
And when you think of the Pharisees listening on the out-
skirts of the crowd that day as this vivid little tale unfolded
itself, and seeing their own dark plots against Him (which
they had imagined were utterly secret) suddenly and dramatically held up to the light before their very faces — when
you think of that, do you not begin to feel that, of all the
brave things Jesus ever did, the telling of this story was one
of the very bravest?

But let us begin at the beginning.

Here was this lord of the vineyard. He bought his ground,

205

planted his vineyard, fenced it round, dug troughs for the wine-press, built a tower, put skilled husbandmen in charge: in short, he did everything conceivable — nothing was omitted or forgotten. Do you remember Isaiah's song of the vineyard? Jesus, steeped in His Old Testament, was remembering and quoting from it here. Listen! 'My beloved hath a vineyard in a very fruitful hill; and he fenced it, and gathered out the stones thereof, and planted it with the choicest vine, and built a tower in the midst of it, and also made a wine-press therein; and he looked that it should bring forth grapes, and it brought forth wild grapes.' And then God's great baffled cry: 'What could have been done more to My vineyard, that I have not done in it?'

Let each of us put this straight to his own soul to-day. What more could God have done for me than what He has done? 'Oh,' cries someone starting up in protest, 'He could have done far more! Look at my narrow lot. God could surely have given me more success, more opportunity, more power and skill and influence and talent, more of the good things of this world.' Yes, perhaps He might. But is there not something deeper? 'There is that soul I have made,' God is saying, and He is looking at someone here as He says it. 'Have I not given him a happy home, and a task to work at; given him parents who prayed for him when he was a child, and friendship with its kindliness, and duty with its challenge; given him eyes to watch the sunset and the splendour of the dawn, ears to hear the glory of noble music, and hands to touch the hem of My garment everywhere; given him the Holy Bible to inspire and kindle his heart, and prayer to keep the road open to the mercy-seat, and all the mystery and majesty of the cross of Christ — what more could I have done for him than what I have done?'

That is the voice of God, our Creator and Redeemer: it is as though God were almost wondering whether He is to blame for the poverty of the result, whether there has been anything lacking on His part. 'What more could I have done?' But today, hearing it, I for one can only answer, 'Nothing, dear God, nothing! Thou hast done everything, more than everything: it is I who am to blame, that the fruit has been so meagre.'

And do you not feel that, too? One of the finest results which this hour of worship could possibly have would be that someone here, before today is done, should kneel down in that quiet room at home, and say, with a meaning in the words that there had never been before:

> 'Spirit of purity and grace,
>   Our weakness, pitying, see;
> O make our hearts Thy dwelling-place,
>   And worthier Thee.'

Look at the parable again, and you will see here a picture of the marvellous patience of God. The lord of the vineyard sends first one servant, and he is beaten; then a second, and he is stoned; then a third, and he is killed; and then 'many others.' In spite of everything, he still keeps on sending them. That is Jesus' picture of Israel's story through the centuries — God sending one prophet after another, God pleading in voice after voice, always hoping that some day at long last His people would listen and repent. But it is not only the story of Israel. It is the story of the soul of man — every man.

When David, away back in the old days, fell into that dreadful disloyalty which smirched his whole career, Providence might have flung the man off, might have said, 'I have done everything I could for him, I found him a shepherd and made him a king, toiled night and day to fashion him into a leader of Israel and a saint, and after all that — this pitiful apostasy! It is heartbreaking. Throw him away!' When Peter and the other disciples began to fight about their stupid little questions of precedence in the very week of the cross, just as though not one of them had ever been with Christ at all or felt His influence in the least degree, He might have wrung His hands in sheer despair. 'You!' He might have cried, 'you to be My witnesses and representatives and ambassadors! After three years with Me, you have not learnt even the first rudimentary lesson, which is love, but act as if nothing I have ever said about this had really been meant at all. No, this finishes it! I am done with you. I will see things through without you.' Was that it? If their Master had been anyone else but Christ, it would have been. But Christ was the incarnate patience of God.

And just think how patient God has been with you and me. Think how many chances He has given us. Think how often, when we have smothered one pleading voice within our heart, He has sent another; and when we have stifled that, He has sent a third; and when we have stoned that to death, He has kept on sending more, and is not worn out with us even yet, but is perhaps sending another to some one here tonight. Think how often, when (as in Jeremiah's picture) the clay of which we are made has snapped and gone to pieces in God's hands, and when He would have been perfectly justified in throwing out such faulty material like rubbish on the scrap-heap, He has done nothing of the kind, but has gathered up the fragments, and started all over again, saying 'I must, I will make something fine and noble of this yet'; refusing to accept any rebuff; crying, when we clench our fist and thrust it up into His face to strike Him, 'Do it again, and again, and again, and I will love you still'; almost, in fact, plaguing us by His patience — it is so dogged and indomitable — frightening us, making us cry, 'God, God, let go! Hands off — don't pester me!' Ah, says a psalmist, if we were to hide in very hell, God would come disturbing us even there. He loves us so much;

and even when we cast Him off, His love keeps remembering happier days when we were truly His.

> 'I will not let thee go.
> The stars that crowd the summer skies
>   Have watched us so below
>   With all their million eyes,
>   I dare not let thee go. . . .
> I hold thee by too many bands:
>   Thou sayest farewell, and lo!
>   I have thee by the hands,
>   And will not let thee go.'

It is to that patience of God, I know without a doubt, that I owe my life and soul. And has not His patience been marvellous with you?

Now notice another fact which Jesus has made very vivid here: the way in which evil always tends to grow. The husbandmen beat the first servant, but when the second came they stoned him, and the third they killed. There you have an instance of the natural and inevitable nemesis of evil. It grows and increases and multiplies itself. Sins apparently trivial open the door to great ones, and these to greater still.

So Cain, in the old story, began with envy; then envy became hatred; then hatred became murder. So Peter had to deny Jesus not once, but thrice; and his first denial was a low, muttered thing, ashamed of itself — 'I do not know Him'; the second was more emphatic, 'I tell you I don't know Him'; the third was a great, terrible shout, with oaths and curses, 'Are you all deaf? Can't you hear me? He is nothing to me — this Jesus — I hate Him!' So in the first verse of the first psalm, you have those three significant verbs, 'walketh, standeth, sitteth': 'Blessed is the man that

walketh not in the counsel of the ungodly' — a mere
casual glance at sin in passing, for the man feels he does not
really belong to that environment, and so he just glances at
it, surreptitiously and half-ashamed and hoping no one
sees him; 'who walketh not,' says the psalmist, 'nor standeth'
— he has halted now, you see, for the sense of shame is going,
and he is growing bolder, and the thing is beginning to
assert itself, to grip; 'walketh, standeth,' and then, finally,
'sitteth,' for the evil has got him now, and he is quite at home
with it — fixed, rooted and settled, belonging to it body and
soul!

That is sin's nemesis: it grows. In the very nature of
things, it is bound to grow. And again and again it has
happened that a man who began by being utterly shocked at
some sin, feeling a shudder pass over his soul at the defiling
contact of it, has ended by saying, 'Sin? Do you call it sin?
I must say I cannot see anything very wrong about it.' Yes,
it grows. It is, as Thomas à Kempis said centuries ago, first
a simple suggestion, then a strong imagination, then delight,
and then assent. And you remember Thackeray's fourfold
progression — an act, a habit, a character, a destiny. That
means that evil is never so easy to destroy as at its first
attack. Then is the time for your soul's ultimatum. Don't
wait, don't parley — be resolute, cast the tempting thought
away. For if once you let it in, it will grow. It cannot help
growing. So it was here. They beat the first servant, stoned
the second, killed the third.

Follow the story further. Here is this lord of the vineyard, with all his messengers rejected and all his appeals
refused; and Luke's version of the parable at this point
represents him as crying, 'What shall I do?' Have you
ever thought of that — God baffled, for the time being at
least, by the blindness of His creatures? More than once
the Scriptures hint at the possibility of that. Take that sudden,

stabbing cry that breaks from one of Hosea's most moving pages: 'O Ephraim, what shall I do unto thee? O Judah, what shall I do unto thee? For your goodness is as a morning cloud, and as the early dew it goeth away.' What a picture of God wringing His hands, as it were, over His wayward children, of God — shall we dare to say it — at His wits' end with men, baulked and thwarted and baffled and bewildered by that sheer dogged dourness that no appeal will move! So here in Jesus' story. 'What shall I do?' cries the Lord of the vineyard, 'what shall I do?'

Then comes the great decision. 'I will send My Son, My well-beloved Son. Surely that will move them! They will reverence My Son.'

Will they? 'We needs must love the highest when we see it,' declares the poet: we cannot help ourselves, we are bound to love it, and to yield to it. Were Christ — so we confidently say — to come back in person to earth today, the whole world would be at His feet. There would be such a revival as has not been seen since Pentecost. Every church would be crowded, every knee bowed in adoration, every voice raised to hail Him King! But do you really think so? Carlyle suggested another possibility: if Jesus returned, He would be — not crucified, oh no! we are not barbarians now — lionised first, fêted and flattered, patronised and invited out to dine, here, there, everywhere, and then — politely ignored! For His demands for utter honesty and reality are still as imperious as ever. When Jesus came back, said Studdert Kennedy, the poet-preacher — for in imagination he had seen it happening —

'they simply passed Him by,
They never hurt a hair of Him, they only let Him die;
For men had grown more tender, and they would not give Him pain,
They only just passed down the street, and left Him in the rain.

Still Jesus cried, 'Forgive them, for they know not what they
  do.'
And still it rained the winter rain that drenched Him through
  and through;
The crowds went home and left the streets without a soul
  to see,
And Jesus crouched against a wall and cried for Calvary.'

'We needs must love the highest': I wonder if that is true.
'They will reverence My Son': I wonder if they will. Let us
narrow this down to the personal point. God is looking at
someone here. He is thinking of you. 'There is a soul,' He is
saying, 'on whom I can count. That soul, seeing My Christ,
will be moved to the depths of his being, will feel everything
that is best within him going down in full surrender, will
forsake sin's last clinging shadows, and stand up and live in
the light!'

Will you? For remember, Christ is God's last appeal.
Refuse this, and you refuse everything. 'Having yet therefore
one Son, His well-beloved, He sent Him last unto them.'
'Here is everything I am,' declares God in the Incarnation,
'here in the fact of Jesus I have bared to you My very heart.'
So that whenever a man faces (as sooner or later he must)
the question 'What shall I do with Jesus?' he is facing life's
ultimate challenge. If this does not move us, nothing will. If
Christ's love does not break us down, God Himself can do no
more. 'They will reverence My Son.' Will you?

It did not happen here. News reaches the rebel servants
in the vineyard that another embassy is on the way. Then
one of their own spies comes running in. 'Do you know who
it is?' he exclaims. 'I have just heard! No ordinary servant
this time — it is the heir, the lord's son!' And at that there is
a clamour of voices. 'His son? The heir?' Then, with a sudden gleam of devilment in their eyes, 'Why then, this is

our chance! As long as he is alive, we shall never be safe, never have this place for our own; but if only he were gone, we could do as we liked, lie as we pleased, and have no one at all to trouble us. See! Yonder he is on the road. We must act — now. Come, let us kill him!' And so when the fearless young messenger arrives, they surround him, set upon him, strike him, fling him down, crush him, trample and batter the life out of him; and then throw the poor dead mangled body outside the vineyard gate.

Just a story, was it? No — but autobiography. For within three days from the telling of the story, the whole thing actually happened. Word for word, the tale came true. For here was Caiaphas, Annas, and the rest, accredited keepers of God's vineyard. And here was the rumour flying around — 'No ordinary prophet, this Man from Nazareth: a greater than a prophet, the Lord's Son!' And here were men obsessed with the thought, 'As long as He lives — this Jesus, this incarnate challenge of God — we shall never be safe. There is going to be no peace for us in our sins, until He has been gagged, silenced, and hurried away out of sight. Come, let us kill Him!' And they did.

And they are doing it still — trying to silence Jesus. They will always be doing it. For Jesus is the most disturbing factor on the face of the earth at this moment. You can't sin in comfort. Christ is there. You can't feel free and happy in your sin: Christ's steady eyes are upon you. You can't call life your own: this stubborn Christ keeps haunting you. And sometimes a man, irked by these feelings and irritated by this Jesus whom he cannot shake off, grows almost desperate, and turns violent hands upon the conscience Christ has kindled within him: he chokes it, suffocates it, shakes the life out of it, and then flings the dead, useless thing away. 'There now,' he tells himself, 'my life is my own at last! I can do what I like in peace.'

But it does not work. For this surely is what the solemn close of the parable means — the final words of the story have the roll of thunder in them — that the most futile thing any man can do is to try to silence God.

Annas, Caiaphas, and the others might rub their hands on the day of Calvary, and say, 'That settles Him! We shall hear no more of Jesus. Just look at Him hanging yonder, dead on His Cross. We have managed this well. He is finished!' Finished? Fools that they were! Everything about him — His life, His influence, His work, His kingdom — had only just begun.

And if they, with Golgotha to help them, could not finish Jesus, no one else can. Stifle the inward voice as much as you please (and how often we do try to stifle it), silence it until you think it gone for ever — and one day it will shatter the silence like a trumpet. Crush down the Christ who haunts you, bury Him beneath years of prayerlessness and neglect — and still He will resurrect Himself, and go marching through your soul. You are never done with Jesus. You have never heard the last of the Son of God. 'Keep we our heads as high as we can,' says Middleton Murry, closing his *Life of Jesus* (and he no orthodox believer, but this is the final verdict to which his study of the fact of Christ constrains him) 'keep we our heads as high as we can, they shall be bowed at the last.' That is the truth. Heaven and earth shall pass away, but His words never. 'Come, let us kill Him, and the vineyard will be ours.' Nay, they killed Him once, and He rose. They have killed Him a hundred times, and a hundred times He has risen. And he is living tonight, and He is here; and of all strange delusions, the strangest, wildest, insanest, is to think that we can get rid of Jesus.

But happily we can finish on another note. Look at the vineyard again, and imagine the scene now changed. The same servants are indeed still there — self-willed, bungling,

unprofitable servants still. The road leading away across
the hills is still there, the road to the land where the Lord of
the vineyard dwells. Once more down the road a solitary
figure can be seen moving. And now the servants (this time
we ourselves are among them) have heard of His coming,
and know who the messenger is. It is the heir to the kingdom,
the Son of the Lord. Now they are waiting for Him at the
gates (and you and I are there), and one thought is filling
every heart — 'His Son? His only Son? Why then, how
greatly He must love us — if, after everything, after all the
sin and all the shame and all the way we have allowed His
vineyard to run to waste, He still thinks us worthy of His
Son! How hugely He must love us, and if He loves like that,
there must be now a new beginning, a new and uttermost
dedication of mind and heart and will, and we must love
Him too.' And now can't you see that solitary figure on the
road drawing near, almost at His journey's end, nearer and
nearer — until the gate is reached? And then, what a shout
it is that rends the skies! 'This is the Heir: come, let us
welcome Him! Son of the Lord of the vineyard, hail!
This is the hour of new beginnings. Hearken, Jesus, to the
vow we make — that never while this vineyard lasts, never
while an ounce of strength abides in us, never while the
memory of Calvary endures, never while life remains, and
love, and honour, and God's voice calling after us down the
winds of all the days and all the nights of our existence —
never will we break our troth to Thee. All hail, Thou Son of
the Lord!'

The True Simplicity

'The simplicity that is in Christ.' — 2 Cor. xi, 3.
'The simplicity that is toward Christ.' — (R.V.)

ONE OF THE MAIN CHARACTERISTICS OF LIFE IN OUR MODERN age is its bewildering complexity. Both outwardly and inwardly, human life is a far more intricate thing today than ever before.

Take its outward aspect. This includes economics, politics, social life, and the like. Economics have grown complex, owing to the innumerable new contacts which have been established between the nations of the earth. Politics have grown complex: national movements, unheard-of twenty years ago, bestride gigantically the scene of history, and democracy struggles for its very existence. Social life has grown complex: for good or ill, there are far more social distractions today than the Victorian Age ever knew.

Or take the more inward aspect of modern life. Everywhere ethical codes are in the melting-pot, religious beliefs are being challenged, and old, inviolable systems of faith and morals which were once unquestioningly accepted as part of the very order of things have come under the onslaught of criticism. Everywhere people are asking: What then, are we to believe? How are we to act? Where are we to find assurance? Both outwardly and inwardly, life is an enormously difficult and complex thing today.

Of course, this complexity has compensating advantages. In economics for instance, every nation is being taught by the very difficulty of the times that never again dare any people imagine that they can stand isolated and self-sufficient in this world; and that discovery is all to the good. In social life, again, the very science which has been responsible for making our age more complex has also opened up for us hundreds of shining gateways, new windows towards knowledge and happiness and fullness of life, which former generations never knew. And in the inner world of the spirit, the growing complexity of our moral and religious problems may imply mean that the new age is refusing to accept, unexamined and at second-hand, traditions and conventions which were largely artificial and unreal, and is determined to think things through for itself; and that again is sheer gain. There are, doubtless, these compensating advantages.

And yet, who does not feel that the growing complexity of life is stealing from us something we can ill afford to lose? The vanishing of the old simplicities is resulting in the disappearance of the old contentment: for science and invention, by ministering to man's pleasures and sensations, have stimulated his demand for these things, and so increased his restlessness. The questioning of the Christian ethical code has had disquieting reactions on the life of home and family. The breakdown of religious conviction has left thousands without a guiding faith of any kind—a fact which largely accounts for the sudden vogue of spiritualism and theosophy. Something of dignity, something of quiet, steadfast simplicity has been stolen from us by this hurrying, complex age; and they may well be pardoned who feel that 'there hath passed away a glory from the earth'.

Here it is worth noticing that the word 'simple' itself is a word which has come down in the world. It has lost caste. When it first appeared, centuries ago, in English literature, it stood for a noble, shining virtue; but no one likes to be called 'simple' today. As originally used, it meant single-hearted, crystal-clear, straightforward. But today the word smacks of its own unfortunate derivative 'simpleton,' and so is under a cloud. Like the other word 'charity' — which from meaning the glowing heart of a genuinely Christian affection has been whittled down till it often signifies a gift which costs the giver nothing and undermines the recipient's self-respect — so the word 'simplicity' has sunk in the world; until people begin to wonder whether to be simple is really a virtue at all.

Yet no writer on this subject has failed to comment on the striking fact that the world's greatest men have invariably been characterised by a deep simplicity of life and character. Tennyson's lines in his 'Ode on the Death of Wellington' are familiar:

> 'Foremost captain of his time,
> Rich in saving common-sense,
> And, as the greatest only are,
> In his simplicity sublime.'

'As the greatest only are,' says Tennyson; and the poet is right. It is the little men who puzzle their biographers to find anything simple about them. The really great men — the Isaiahs, the Pauls, the Bunyans, the Wilberforces — have been at heart as simple as children. And that is true also of those who, although their names never appear on any roll of fame, are nevertheless great in God's sight — utterly obscure and unknown to men, yet great in character. A man may be a saint without many of the qualities which this complex world ranks high; no man can be a saint without a deep simplicity of soul.

Now it is a law of life that every prevalent mood sooner or later provokes a reaction; and therefore it is not surprising that in this complex age we hear a good deal about the 'craving for a simple life'. It was that craving which periodically drove Marie Antoinette out from the pomp and cir-

cumstance of a decadent luxury to play at being a farm-girl
in the rustic solitudes of Versailles. It is that craving which
takes a great part of our population for a week or two in
the year from the desk, the shop, the factory; which puts a
pack on a man's back and a staff in his hand, and sets his
face to the open road and the heather and the hills and
Nature's great simplicities. It is that craving of which a
hundred poets have sung:

'London streets are gold — ah, give me leaves a glinting
    'Midst grey dykes and hedges in the autumn sun!
London's water's wine, poured out for all unstinting —
    God! For the little brooks that tumble as they run!'

But the craving for a simple life goes deeper than all this:
and you can see from history how a complex, sophisticated
age always brings on a reaction. Inevitably the pendulum
swings back. There comes a turn of the tide. So it was when
St. Anthony of Egypt, sickened by the worldliness and vice
of the great pagan cities around him, cut the cables, sacrificed
all his wealth and standing, and made his home in the desert.
So it was again when St. Francis of Assisi led his little band
of friars out from the moral and social entanglements of
mediaeval Italy into something like the joy and freedom of
first-century Galilee. So it was most dramatically when
Martin Luther, leading on the Reformation, cut at one
stroke through the complex casuistry of papal doctrine and
gave back to the individual soul the directness and immediacy
of true religion. And in our own day there are signs that
another recoil from over-elaboration is on the way, another
reversion to a truer simplicity beginning to make itself felt;
taking the form, in social life, of a new distaste and nausea of
the endless catering for sensation; in moral life, of a new
Puritanism which is not going to allow life's sanctities to be
dragged in the mud indefinitely by writers of mean and

petty soul; and in religious life, of a new evangelicalism which, weary of hair-splitting dialectic and endless argument, is ready to cry to the purveyors of these things — 'Stand out of the way, and let us through to God!'

We have to guard here, however, against a false simplicity. That there is such a thing, there can be no doubt. It is possible, for example, to aim at a false simplicity in our social life. Suppose we resolved to give up our gains of science and invention, out steam and electricity and antiseptic surgery, and make ourselves thoroughly primitive again. Clearly we should be going against the will of God. For that would be the line of retrogression, not of advance. Again, it is possible to have a false simplicity in our moral life. We could make things easier and much more manageable for ourselves by narrowing down our sphere of interests, cutting out certain instincts and desires altogether, and timidly giving everything dangerous a wide berth. But that is not the simplicity God wants to see us achieving. That is just evading the battle. Once again, it is possible to have a false simplicity in our religious life. We might cry, as some are doing, 'Give us a religion without theology, without mystery, without any demand on thought and reason!' But that most emphatically is not the simplicity into which God seeks to lead us. It was Henry Drummond who said he did not congratulate, he pitied, the man who was cocksure of everything in his faith. Let it be repeated: there is a false simplifying of our complex life which is worse than useless.

But some simplification must surely be possible. There must be some way — even though all the social, moral, and religious perplexities of this present age are clamouring in our ears — some way of keeping our own lives uncontaminated and poised and simple. Where are we to find that way? Paul has got hold of it here in our text. 'The simplicity,' he says, 'that is in Christ.'

It is very important that we should remark the difference which the Revised Version has introduced. The Revised Version says 'the simplicity that is *toward* Christ'; and that is almost certainly the right rendering. That is what the apostle meant — not primarily the simplicity that was in Jesus Himself, and that marked His earthly life; but the simplicity which ought to be in the hearts of those who love and trust and follow Him, the harmony and poise and unity of a character steel-true and blade-straight, the consistency of an undivided loyalty to the Lord of all good life. That is Paul's meaning. But let us, ere we pass, accept the old translation for a moment; for even if it was not what the apostle said, it does represent a real fact.

'The simplicity that is in Jesus.' Think how simple the earthly life of Jesus was — this peasant Christ, who while He lived had nowhere to lay His head, and when He died left behind Him as His only possession the seamless robe He wore. When will the world learn from Jesus' life the great lesson that between riches on the one hand and happiness on the other there is no necessary connection whatever? There have been rich people in this world who have been happy; but where that has been the case, it has not been their riches that made them happy, but something else altogether — something in character quite independent of every question of worldly possessions: Christ Jesus, Carpenter of Nazareth, Child of Mary, is a living confutation of the philosophy of life that connects wealth and happiness, and a standing rebuke to the pampered artificiality of a great deal of life today.

'Love had he found in huts where poor men lie,
    His daily teachers had been woods and rills, —
The silence that is in the starry sky,
    The sleep that is among the lonely hills.'

Again, think how simple the speech of Jesus was. 'The common people,' we are told, 'heard Him gladly.' They did not hear their own Rabbis gladly. Their own Rabbis only fogged their minds, and blurred the issues, and spoke above their heads. But when Jesus spoke it was all so practical that they could connect it up at once with their own experience; it was so straight that none could miss its meaning; it was so concrete that it came on them as a glorious discovery after the weary abstractions to which their Rabbis had persistently treated them. Remember that simplicity of speech is a very different thing from superficiality of thought. The simplest language is often the profoundest, and every man who listened knew that Jesus was striking home to the very deepest things in life. Shallow in speech Jesus could never be: yet, by the grace of God, He was utterly simple always.

Or think, again, how simple was the salvation which Jesus offered. 'Follow Me,' He said, and that was all. And how simple the cross is! Indeed, the very simplicity of the gospel has been, in the eyes of many, its condemnation. They tell you it is a much too simple philosophy for this intricate life — just to 'trust and obey.' They declare that this tangled, chaotic world needs something more than to be told that 'there is life for a look at the Crucified One.' Hence in the twentieth century you have the amazing spectacle of men trying to improve upon the means of grace that God Himself has devised. Hence you have religion cluttered up with all kinds of unnecessary accretions. Hence you have good, earnest people narrowing down the way of salvation to their own particular mode of it — whether it be Presbyterian or Anglican or Methodist or Roman Catholic — and treating their own preferences, their own accepted historic religious forms, as part of the very essence of the gospel, without which there can be no salvation. But surely all that spirit is terribly unlike Jesus! 'Whosoever will, let him come.' That is the gospel — as welcoming as two wide-open arms, as simple as a cross.

But above all, think how simple Jesus was in His own soul. However worrying life was, He never grew distracted; however loud its voices, He never felt dismay; however threatening its dangers, He walked in perfect peace. And the secret? Christ Himself has let us into His secret. It was His undivided loyalty to God. 'My meat,' He said, 'is to do the will of Him that sent Me.' There you have the one claim to which all rival claims were subservient, the one principle co-ordinating the whole of life, the one standard by reference to which every question as it arose was decided— an undivided loyalty to the God of heaven. That was Christ's great simplification of life. And it works.

It can work for us, in our own crowded, jostling age. And this is where the Revisers, with their flash of insight, come in: 'the simplicity that is *toward* Christ!' Do you understand the secret now? Here is the answer to the deep craving for the simple life — an undivided loyalty, a heart fixed utterly on Christ, and through Christ on God.

The simplicity that is towards Jesus! Do not let us blame the complexity of the age, if our lives have lost the simple note. It is not the fault of the age; it is our own fault; it is the nemesis of trying to serve more than one master. We have been hoping to have life both ways — God's way and our own way; and it cannot be done. Divided loyalties are the death of simplicity: they lead to endless complications. But see what happens when Christ comes in as the one controlling principle. Whenever a problem arises in your life, you have now one standard to refer it to for decision; whenever any anxiety threatens you have one unfailing refuge; and whenever rival claims grow loud, you have one Commander-in-chief of your soul to give the final ruling. That is the great simplification of life, that is the Golden

Age come back again — an undivided heart at Jesus' feet.

The late Bishop Moule has told how once during the War, at the close of a variety entertainment given in London for men going out to the Front, a young officer rose, at his Colonel's request, to express the men's thanks. He did so in genial words of charm and humour. Then suddenly, as if in afterthought, and in a different tone, he added: 'We are soon crossing to France and to the trenches, and very possibly, of course, to death. Will any of our friends here tell us how to die?' There was a long, strained silence. No one knew what to say. But then the answer came. One of the singers made her way quietly forward to the front of the stage, and began to sing the great aria from the *Elijah*, 'O Rest in the Lord.' There were few dry eyes when the song was done.

Here, above all else, is what each one of us needs in the battle of life — a heart that has come to rest in God, a will fully surrendered. That is the great secret. That is the final simplification. That alone will bring us through with honour.

XXIII

A Drama in Four Acts

'Take Mark, and bring him with thee: for he is profitable to me for the ministry.' — 2 TIMOTHY iv. 11.

THE STORY OF JOHN MARK, THE DESERTER WHO MADE GOOD, could be written as a drama in four acts. But first, by way of prologue to the drama, a question arises. How came Mark to be accompanying Paul and Barnabas on their hazardous adventures? This is easily enough explained. There are three facts to remember.

The first is that Barnabas was his own cousin, and was no doubt eager to give the younger man a share in the great work of carrying Christ's commission across the world.

The second is that John Mark came from a home which had played an outstanding part in the life of the Church from the first. His mother, Mary, had put her house at the disposal of the Jerusalem Christians. It was there, in an upper room of her house, that they met for weekly worship. It was thither that Peter had made his way on his dramatic escape from prison. Indeed, the probability is that it was this same upper room which had seen the Last Supper on the night of Calvary, and the coming of the Spirit at Pentecost, and the birth of the Christian Church. Mark was the son of that home. Happy the young man who begins life in a home where God has an altar and Jesus is a familiar friend!

But we can go farther. The third fact is that it is at least possible that Mark himself had been a secret disciple of Jesus. You will remember how his Gospel, when it comes to describe Gethsemane, mentions a mysterious young man who was in the garden on the night when Jesus was arrested, who was almost arrested himself, and escaped only by fleeing and leaving his cloak behind him in the soldiers' hands. None of the other evangelists mentions the incident, and tradition says that the young man was Mark himself, who put this personal touch into his Gospel like an artist painting in his signature very faintly in an inconspicuous corner of his picture. However that may be, it is certain that he had been in close touch with the Christian leaders from the first. Hence we are not surprised to find him setting out with Paul and Barnabas on the first great gospel campaign.

So we pass on from the prologue to Act I of the drama. This act bears the title *Recantation*. To begin with, all went well. Mark felt he had found his vocation. There was all the glamour of novelty about it — new places to visit, new friendships to make, new claims to stake out for Christ, But as the days went on, one thought began to trouble him. Were they not wandering too far from their base? Paul with his far horizons and beckoning visions, seemed determined to carry the campaign into the unfamiliar and dangerous hinterland of Asia. Now Mark had not bargained for this. 'The risk is far too great,' he told himself, 'it is not worth it! I must remonstrate with Paul.' But when he endeavoured to raise his objections, he found that he could scarce say a word, for there was something in Paul's face, a burning, passionate eagerness and a glowing resolute determination, which silenced his stammered protests; and there seemed no alternative — he must go on. But all the time his nerve was beginning to fail him, and he knew it. What a wild, savage, God-forsaken land this was, and up among those mountain fastnesses what nameless perils might be lurking! And Jerusalem was so far away; and his heart so terribly homesick! Many a night he would have given anything just to have heard the Temple bells again, or to have stood on Olivet and seen the sun flaming down the western sky. So the struggle went on in Mark's soul, till at last there came a crisis.

It was in the dead of night, and Paul and Barnabas were asleep; but Mark was wakeful, and was striding up and down alone by himself in the dark. Take a long look at him, I beg you — for there is a man at the crossroads with Christ, a soul facing one of those decisive hours that come to all of us sooner or later. 'I can't go on,' he is saying. 'I ought never to have come. O home, home — I'm weary for my home!'

And then another voice speaks, very quietly and tenderly, and it is the voice of Jesus.

'You are not going to leave Me, My friend? You surely can't be leaving Me now? Do you not love Me any more?'

And the man blurts out, 'Yes, Lord I do, you know I do! With all my heart I love you. How can you say such a thing? But, Lord, I don't think I was built for this. I'm not a Paul or a Barnabas, I'm not like them with their iron nerves and their lion hearts — I'm just one of your ordinary people, Jesus: and it is asking too much of me!'

Then again the quiet voice speaks, but sadly now — 'I do not compel you, friend. You are free to return if you must. But I died for you, My son, and this is hard, hard for Me!'

'But don't you see, Lord, I can't go on? You must see that. I have tried my best, I had indeed, but I am not made for this kind of life, and it is not fair to ask me. Can't you understand?'

And at that a new voice, a third voice, comes breaking in — the voice of the Tempter.

'Let Christ go, then. Let Him go! Sell Him and be done with it. Recant, man, recant!'

And then a great silence. But in the morning, when Paul and Barnabas rose to continue their journey, there was no John Mark there. And they went on their way alone. The tragedy of a soul's recantation!

Now I know what some of us are thinking. All this was long, long ago. Conditions have changed completely. Christian discipleship is a far simpler affair today: no danger of our deserting Christ through fear!

But are we sure? Suppose we single out one particular brand of fear. What about the fear of unpopularity, of being left on the shelf (as we say), of being passed over or made to suffer for our convictions? Does that never breed deserters?

Let me for one moment speak directly to the young men and women here tonight. Have you never stood at this particular cross-roads with Christ, finding yourself suddenly confronted with the choice either to stand up for Jesus and let the world's good graces go, or else to muffle your Christianity and square the world and keep the favour of some social set? Perhaps you had only five minutes or less to make up your mind, to decide whether the flag was to be run to the top of the mast and held there resolutely in defiance of the consequences, or discreetly hauled down and pushed away out of sight. 'Men of Athens,' exclaimed Socrates, 'I hold you in the highest reverence and love; but I am going to obey God rather than you!' It takes some courage to do that, in this modern age as much as in ancient Athens. It takes some grit and loyalty to do it — in social circle, or shop, or factory, or club. When Wilberforce rose to speak in the House of Commons, 'Ah,' said a sneering member, 'the honourable and religious gentleman!' That sort of thing stings; and there is a bit of us — 'the natural man', Paul called it — which hates being stung, and would rather do anything, would even blunder into open disloyalty and sin against God's Christ than stand out against the conventions of the world or the opinion of our fellow men. Unpopularity — that is one fear at least which still has the power to make souls desert from Christ. And there are others, the fear of sacrifice, for example, the fear of losing ambitions on which our hearts are set, the fear of having to give up something in thought, desire, or habit which we know ought to be given up (this is one of the sternest struggles of life, and until a man has fought through it he is not right with Christ), the fear of God's daily discipline, the fear of the cross. Is there one of us here who will dare point a condemning finger at John Mark, or cast the first stone? Are we not all in this together? Yes, in some degree we have all played our part in this first tragic act — the act of recantation.

We go on now to Act II; and this bears the title *Remorse*. Here we see Mark back in Jerusalem. The homesick man has come home. Away yonder among the mountains of Asia he had thought, 'If only I could see Jerusalem, how happy I should be!' Well, here he is in Jerusalem. Is he happy now? Look at him.

People sometimes say a house is haunted. Perhaps, years before, some dark deed was perpetrated there; and the place has never thrown off its evil, sinister reputation. No prospective tenants come knocking at its door. It stands deserted and uncared for, and weeds and nettles block the garden paths. Passers-by cast furtive glances at it in the daytime, and in the night the wind moans eerily around its walls, like the moaning of the ghosts of the dead. So sometimes the house of life, the soul, is haunted; and ghosts of memory walk there, clanking their chains in the dark, shadows of old unhappy far-off things and wild regrets.

'In the night, in the night
 When thou liest alone,
 Ah! the ghosts that make moan
From the days that are sped:
 The old dreams, the old deeds,
 The old wound that still bleeds,
And the face of the dead,
 In the night.'

That was John Mark, back in Jerusalem. Everything was the same — the streets, his home, the Temple bells, the sun flaming down behind Olivet, everything the same: yet somehow there was a subtle difference. All the dear familiar things had lost their savour. Happy in Jerusalem? Call him rather the most wretched man on earth. After recantation, remorse. Does it not always happen? Thomas Cranmer, Archbishop of Canterbury in the sixteenth century, recanted his faith in prison. 'Sign that!' they said to him, thrusting a written document into his hands. But when he began to read it, 'Nay,' he burst out, ''tis a downright denial of my Christ! I will not sign.' 'Sign it or die,' they threatened, and kept badgering him and torturing him, till in a weak moment he yielded, and took the pen and wrote his name. But when it was done, the horror of his betrayal leapt upon his soul, and he looked at the right hand that had signed the name. Had not Jesus said, 'If thy hand offend thee, cut it off'? And for days and nights he was tormented with remorse. He would gladly have taken a knife, and severed that traitor hand. And when at last, in spite of his recantation, they led him out to die, and the vast throng swarmed round the martyr pyre to see the end, he stood and thrust his right arm first into the flames. 'This unworthy hand,' he said, 'this which hath sinned, having signed the writing, must be the first to suffer,' and he held it there till it was blackened and consumed; then plunged into the fire himself.

Words cannot measure the remorse that gripped John Mark in Jerusalem; but the grip of it was agony. 'Would God I might live those days through again!' he thought. 'If only the thing had never happened! O God of mercy, turn time back, I beg, set me where I was before this dreadful thing occurred. I can't have been myself then! For I do love Jesus. I swear I love Him still. Lord, give me that bad hour back!'

One of Squire's fine poems depicts a man who has per-

sistently neglected a dear one. Always he has been meaning
to write, to send the long-looked-for letter; and always in
the press of business he has kept putting it off. 'Tomorrow I
will do it,' he tells himself, 'certainly I will write tomorrow';
but it is never done. And then one day a message comes. He
tears it open: she is dead. And as he stands there, staring at
the words, remorse rushes in like a flood. 'It shall not be
today,' he cries. 'It shall not! It is still yesterday. I'll
wrest the sun back in its course! It is still yesterday.
There is time still — there must be time!' Poor, unhappy
soul! For

> 'The sun moves. Our onward course is set.
>   There will be time for nothing but regret,
>   And the memory of things done!'

'You don't know,' cries the chaplain in Shaw's *Saint Joan*,
breaking in wildly after he had consented to the saint's
death and had stood and watched her die, 'you haven't seen:
it is so easy to talk when you don't know. But when it is
brought home to you; when you see the thing you have
done; when it is blinding your eyes, stifling your nostrils,
tearing your heart, then — then — O God, take away this
sight from me! O Christ, deliver me from this fire that is
consuming me! She cried to Thee in the midst of it: Jesus!
Jesus! Jesus! She is in Thy bosom; and I am in hell for
evermore.'

After recantation — remorse!

So with John Mark. I think I can see him at night,
unable to sleep, rising from his bed, pacing to and fro in that
upper room of many memories. 'Where are Paul and
Barnabas tonight?' he is wondering. 'And where is Jesus?'
I see him going down a Jerusalem street at noonday, and
now and again people — Christian brethren of his own —
look strangely at him as he passes, then turn and point: 'See,

there is the man who deserted! Would you believe it?' I see him at last one day sitting at the Communion table. He is listening dully to the familiar words, 'This is My body, broken for you. This is My blood, shed for you'; and then the bread comes round, and then the cup. But just as he lifts it, something happens. He pauses, and looks at that cup in his hand, for within him a voice has begun to speak — a voice unheard by any of the others there, heard only in Mark's own soul. 'This is Christ's blood,' says the voice. 'And if this is blood in the cup, and if it is the blood of Jesus, and if it was given for you, then what — in the name of all that is honourable — are you doing here? Jesus is out on the lonely, dangerous ways, seeking the lost and the perishing, and this is the blood of that agony. Will you dare to drink it — you? Look well into that cup, Mark, for you are crucifying Christ afresh, and there are drops of the blood of that second crucifixion in it. Look well into the cup!' And the man sits with the cup in his hand, staring at it (have we ever sat like that, confronted with the agony of Jesus, and knowing that some unclean thought of ours, some selfish slackness, some wretched little self-indulgence, was the cause of it?) and then I see him suddenly setting the cup down untasted, rising from the table, and leaving the room — and that very night, do you know where he is? Out from Jerusalem, out on the great North road, with his face set towards Paul and Barnabas and Christ again!

There is an old Gaelic proverb which says, 'If you cannot get back to the place where you were born, try to get within seeing distance of it.' I would add to that: If you cannot get back to the place where you were first born into the life in God, get within seeing distance of it. Jesus Christ will do the rest.

So we come to Act III: and the title of this is *Restoration*. You know the story — how Mark returned to Paul and

Barnabas; how Barnabas welcomed him eagerly, but Paul refused to have anything to do with him (surely if Jesus had been there, it would have been Barnabas's way, not Paul's, He would have taken); how that unhappy dispute led to a quarrel, and the quarrel to a parting, Barnabas going off with Mark, and Paul with Silas; how this splendid coward redeemed his reputation, and proved himself a true hero of Christ, so that even Paul relented in the end, and took him to his heart again; and how when the great apostle lay awaiting his death in Rome, it was of Mark that he kept thinking. 'Take Mark,' he wrote to Timothy, 'and bring him with thee; for he is profitable to me for the ministry.'

That is the familiar story. And this is the blessed and most glorious truth which it stands to announce to all who have ears to hear: the past can be blotted out. The heaviest and most shameful burden beneath which any soul in the world is staggering now is not too heavy for Jesus to deal with, nor too shameful for Him to take up in His pierced, royal hands and cast finally away — so that the soul which has gone lame and hirpling under it for years will never set eyes on it again!

It would be a great thing — the gospel of Jesus — even if it applied only to those who had fought the good fight and run the straight race all their lives. But blessed be God, it is more than that, far more; and if the Christian preacher and evangelist has the gladdest and most thrilling task in all the world, it is because he has been authorized by God to proclaim the forgiveness of sins, the removing of their guilt and the shattering of their power. What *is* the gospel? Hope for the hopeless, love for the unlovable, heroism for the most arrant coward, white shining robes for the raggedest, clean-hearted purity for the muddiest, inward peace and a great serenity for spirits torn and frantic with regret. There is a most moving scrap of conversation in George Macdonald's

Robert Falconer. 'If only I knew that God was as good
as that woman, I should be content.' 'Then you don't believe
that God is good?' 'I didn't say that, my boy. But to know
that God was good and kind and fair — heartily, I mean,
and not half-ways with ifs and buts. My boy, there would be
nothing left to be miserable about.' Believe me, if you have
once seen Jesus, as the men and women of the New Testament saw Him, there *is* nothing left to be miserable about.
There is everything in the world to set you singing! And if
I were to stand here and preach to you a limited gospel; if
I were to tell you of a Christ who is the Lover of some elect,
sky-blue souls who have never known the bitterness of self-
despising and remorse, but not the Lover of all the world; if
I were to suggest that there are depths of shame and humiliation and defeat from which the heights of heaven cannot be
stormed; if I were to hedge God's lovingkindness round with
ifs and buts and reservations and conditions — I should be
preaching a lie. 'Him that cometh to Me I will in no wise
cast out.' Was Jesus shocked when He saw them coming?
Did Jesus ever turn round and say, 'Ah, I did not mean you!
I can go down deep to rescue the perishing, but not quite
to such depths as that'? No, He saw them coming, lame and
lost and lonely and sin-scarred and disillusioned and miserable, and He lifted up His eyes to heaven: 'I thank Thee,
Father, Lord of heaven and earth, that the gospel of grace
works even here! I thank Thee that Thou hast sent Me to
restore to these Thy broken children the years that the locust
hath eaten.' And He took them to His arms, God's bairns
who had got hurt, and let them sob the whole sad story out:
and then — 'That is finished,' He said, 'behold, I make all
things new.' Do we today believe it? Take your own life,
take the saddest recantation there has ever been, take the
most locust-eaten year you can remember, take the thing
which may be hiding God for you at this very moment. Lay
that at Christ's feet. Say, 'Lord, if Thou wilt —!' And see if,

for you, the ancient miracle is not renewed, and the whole world filled with glory.

And so we end with Act IV of Mark's story. We have watched his recantation and his remorse, and then his restoration. The title which this final act bears is *Reparation*. One thing only let me say in closing. How did Mark atone? How did he repair the damage he had done? He became an evangelist. He wrote a book. He gave the world a Life of Jesus, the first Gospel to be written. We can be sure of this, that multitudes of people in those old, far-off days, who had never seen Jesus in the flesh, met Him in the pages of Mark's book, and entered — under the evangelist's guidance — upon the highroad leading to salvation. And still today after all these years Mark is introducing men and women of every race and religion to Jesus, and setting them face to face with the redeeming Son of God. That was his atonement. Was it not a glorious reparation?

What, then, of ourselves? We who have wounded Christ so often — is there any reparation we can offer? We cannot be evangelists like Mark, we say. It is not given to us to write Gospels for the world to read. But think again! Is it not? The fact is, there is not one of us here today who cannot compose a life of Jesus. You can write an evangel, not in books and documents, but in deeds and character. You can make men see Jesus. You can live in such a way that, even when you are not speaking about religion at all, you will be confronting souls with Christ — His ways, His spirit, His character — and making them feel the power and the beauty of the Son of God. And it may be that, all unknown to you, one soul here or another there will owe its very salvation to that gospel of yours; it may be that someone will rise from among the throngs around the judgment-seat on the last day, and pointing at you will cry: 'There is the man to whom, under God, I owe everything! It was reading

the gospel of Christ in that man's life that redeemed me.'
And Jesus will turn to you with glad and grateful eyes. 'Come
ye blessed of My Father — inherit the kingdom!'

XXIV

The Close of an Epoch[1]

'He hath shewed thee, O man, what is good; and what
doth the Lord require of thee, but to do justly, and to
love mercy, and to walk humbly with thy God?' —
MICAH. vi. 8.

WE MEET HERE THIS MORNING FOR OUR COMMUNION
celebration, under the shadow of an Empire's bereavement.
Little could we foresee, when we remembered our King last
Sunday, and sang our National Anthem, little could we
contemplate the circumstances in which we are gathered
today. 'He asked life of Thee,' says the psalmist, 'and
Thou gavest it him, even length of days for ever and
ever.'

You will not expect me this morning to speak any words
of official homage: this loss, to all of us, is much too personal for that. I wonder if anyone could sit, last Monday
night at half-past nine, listening to the poignant words from
London, 'The King's life is moving peacefully towards its
close,' without an acute sense of personal and private grief,
as if it were on our own homes, our own family circle, that
the blow were falling?

There came to my mind some beautiful words of Donald
Hankey who died in the War. They are in his essay, *The
Beloved Captain*, 'We were his men, and he was our leader.
There was a bond of mutual confidence between us, which
grew stronger and stronger as the months passed. The fact
was that he had won his way into our affections. We loved

[1]Preached on the Sunday following the death of King George V.

him. And there isn't anything stronger than love, when all's said and done.' Of King George V. of Britain, how deeply true that is!

It was in the Jubilee rejoicings that that love found its chance of expression. Never surely can there have been more convincing proof that a King had come into his own! Never did monarch receive more touching or more thrilling evidence of a people's devotion. He knew then how absolutely and finally and unreservedly they had given him their heart.

Consider his achievement. In a generation when throughout the world thrones have been tottering and dynasties falling, he has left his throne stronger than ever. In days of unexampled strain and difficulty, his courage never faltered. The most democratic monarch this land has ever had, he has impressed his personality on the life of the nation.

It must be the loneliest thing on earth, to be a King. And yet, perhaps — not altogether lonely, when someone stands beside him. We think today, with millions of others, of Queen Mary in her widowhood. We thank God for the pillar of strength that she has been throughout the quarter of a century of the reign now closed. And to our lips, for her, there comes the poet's prayer —

> 'The love of all thy people comfort thee
> Till God's love set thee at his side again.'

I have chosen the words from Micah for our text today, for it seems to me that they might stand as an epitome of our late King's life. 'He hath shewed thee, O man, what is good; and what doth the Lord require of thee, but to do justly, and to love mercy, and to walk humbly with thy God?' There the prophet has singled out the three great elements of the complete and rounded life — doing justly, that is, sympathy of heart; and walking humbly with God, that is, reverence of spirit. Our monarch had them all.

What doth the Lord require of thee, but *to do justly*? He was, to borrow Tennyson's phrase about Queen Victoria 'loyal to the royal in himself' — a character of sterling integrity.

Think of his sense of duty. How devotedly, how sacrificially, he gave himself to the overwhelmingly arduous labours of his high station, toiling often beyond his allotted strength!

Think, too, how he exalted the domestic virtues; how he took the old word 'Home' — which, alas! so many in this generation affect to despise and disregard — how he took it, and honoured it, and lifted it high; and how, by so doing, he set a standard for all social and public life, and made his own life at once an inspiration and a challenge to all his subjects.

Such a life indeed reminds us that character alone is the true wealth. It is a reminder that we constantly require. It is so easy, under the influence of the spirit of the age and the pressure of society, to become almost unconsciously infected by the doctrine that 'man *can* live by bread alone'; to follow the crowd in believing that cleverness, astuteness, and worldly wisdom are the qualities that matter most; to set rights above duties, self-interest above self-sacrifice, and success above simple sincerity of soul. But if 'man looketh on the outward appearance, the Lord looketh on the heart.' And as the late Rudyard Kipling put it to the St. Andrews students in his fine Rectorial on *Independence*: 'A man may be festooned with the whole haberdashery of success, and go to his grave a castaway.' The one thing that lasts is character. The one thing that matters is what a man is, when his soul stands naked and alone before its God. Over and over again the Bible bids us remember, gives this indeed as

the final truth about life, that 'the world passeth away' —
and those who make the world their horizon pass and are
swept away with it — 'but he that doeth the will of God — he
alone — abideth forever.'

The second element of the complete and rounded life
which the prophet has singled out is this, 'What doth the
Lord require of thee, but *to love mercy*?' If the first was
integrity of character, this is sympathy of heart.

Nothing endeared our late King to his people more than
his amazingly broad human sympathy. Take one little
wartime story — a story that speaks volumes. A young
New Zealand soldier had been terribly wounded. He was
lying in a casualty clearing station just behind the lines. It
was at a time when King George was on one of his many visits
to the Western front, and he chanced to enter the place
where the dying boy lay. He moved slowly from one stretcher
to another, saying a few kind words beside each. Meanwhile
the Young New Zealander was watching him, with a puzzled
look in his eyes, as though he were wondering, 'Who is that
man? Where have I seen him before? Or where have I seen
his picture?' But when the stranger came and stood beside
his own stretcher, into the puzzled eyes a flash of recognition
came. The dying lad reached out a weak hand, and mur-
mured, 'I've heard of you, sir — put it there,' that simple
instinctive gesture — what impressive testimony to the
humanity behind the royalty, the man behind the King, a
man with deepest grace of sympathy, a man of a great
understanding heart!

It was this, perhaps more than anything, that won him
the confidemce of his people. The familiar words, 'Bear ye
one another's burdens, and so fulfil the law of Christ,' were
to King George no mere beautiful maxim: they were a daily
act of self-dedication. What it cost him to bear that burden,
none will know; but always his people knew that it was being

borne. They knew that he would never be at rest, while any of them were labouring under poverty or squalor or injustice. They knew he understood what life was to the poor and the handicapped, the unemployed and the struggling and the unhappy. They knew that in all their afflictions he was afflicted — their burdens his burden, their anxieties his anxiety, their troubles his trouble. Not of every monarch has this been true. Not even of every monarch in our own country's history has this been true. Some have been excluded from sharing their people's life by lack of imagination: others, through lack of inclination have excluded themselves. But he whom we mourn today has been a veritable father of his people. His fellow-feeling with his subjects brought him their confidence and affection. His sympathy made him great.

Let us, as we sit at our Communion Table today, ask the good God to fill us with the sympathy of Christ. There is such a desperate famine for sympathy in this old world today. Pass along the streets, mingle with the crowds, sit among a worshipping congregation — there are far more 'men of sorrows and acquainted with grief' around you than the surface appearance of things would show. And when you think of what ordinary folk have to endure in this world, and are enduring every day, do not begin to feel that the hard spirit, the superior spirit, the censorious spirit, is not just a mistake, but the very essence of sin, and downright enmity with Christ? As Lacordaire, the great French preacher, used to put it — 'Be kind: it is so like God!'

'O ye who taste that love is sweet,
 Set waymarks for all doubtful feet
 That stumble on in search of it.'

'What doth God require of thee, but to love mercy?'

The third and final element of the complete and rounded

life which the prophet has singled out is this, 'What doth He require of thee, but *to walk humbly with thy God*?' 'To do justly — to love mercy — to walk humbly with God': if the first was integrity of character, and the second sympathy of heart, this is reverence of spirit.

No tribute to our late King can be anything but totally inadequate and false that ascribes his faithfulness in duty and his loving service of his people to any other source than his religion. That was the secret of his life.

It is not unknown for persons in authority and in official positions to use the word 'God' merely officially and glibly. There was the expression of a firm personal faith and an intense religious conviction.

You will remember — who now can ever forget? — One sentence in the last Christmas message he broadcast to his people. Speaking of the Empire's respect for the throne, he added the words — 'and for the man himself who, may God help him, has been placed upon it.' That, in very truth, throughout the quarter of a century of his reign, was the source from which the daily help for his tremendous task was drawn. That explains the genesis of all his many acts and gestures of kindness and self-forgetfulness, those deeds which would never have occurred to anyone to do who was not in touch with the Spirit of Christ. His help was in the name of the Lord who made heaven and earth. He walked humbly with his God.

From this sprang his devotion to the Scriptures and to the public worship of the Church. We have all heard how, as far back as the year 1881, the young Prince who was to become our King gave his word to Queen Alexandra that he would read a chapter of the Bible daily, and how through all his life, on to its very close, he faithfully adhered to that promise. And never surely was there a monarch of this land who could take the psalmist's words more sincerely upon his lips — 'I was glad when they said unto me, Let us go into the house of the Lord'. We ought to thank God that in a generation when so many, in every walk of life, have thrown off the ancient pieties of prayer and praise and worship, and have chosen to turn the Lord's Day to their own uses, with never one thought of Christ and never one word of gratitude to the grace that has given them their life — we ought to thank God that we have been ruled over by one who bore such consistent witness and gave such noble example.

Let such a life remind us that there is one great steadfast Rock for our slipping feet amid the storms and chaos of these times — and that is the Word of God in Holy Scripture, where whosoever will can hold converse with the saints and hear the message of the King of kings. Let it remind us that prayer is the Christian's vital breath; and that the Lord's Day has been given us to ensure that amid all the rush and fever and fret and dust and heat of crowded days we may receive a new vision of the things that are spiritual and eternal, that vision without which the people perish. 'O that Scotland,' cried Samuel Rutherford in the great days of the Covenanters, 'that Scotland, all with one shout, would cry up Christ, and that His name were high in this land!' Above all, let it remind us of this, that if the great assertions of our Christian creed are true — if there is one God over all the earth; if there is a Son of God calling us to rise and follow; if there is a Spirit of God speaking in our conscience, convicting and convincing; if there is a Kingdom of God that shall outlast the stars; if there is an Eternity of God towards which we all are moving; if there is a Throne of God before which we shall stand to give account, when this earthly life is done; if these things which we say we believe are more than pious sentiments, if they are facts, then they are incomparably the most important facts with which everyone of us has to reckon, implying, nay demanding, that we make religion the masterforce of all our life, and God in Christ the burning centre of our being. 'What doth the Lord require of thee, but to walk humbly with thy God?'

> 'O for a closer walk with God,
>   A calm and heavenly frame,
> A light to shine upon the road
>   That leads me to the Lamb!'

So to our good and gracious and God-fearing King, we give now our 'hail and farewell.' In a moment we shall be singing that hymn which of all hymns he held the dearest, the hymn which those who knew him tell us he could never sing without emotion:

> 'O Love that wilt not let me go,
>   I rest my weary soul in Thee.'

Our comfort, while we sing it, will be this, that of him it is now so splendidly and so royally true: his soul, weary with the almost crushing burden of his high and lonely station, has found its full release, in the rest that remaineth for the people of God.

Come, then, with gladness mingling with your sorrow, come to the Table of Jesus Christ. Come to this hallowed spot where the cloud of witnesses gathers, and the communion of the saints grows real. Come, in the name of free grace and dying love and life eternal. Come with new resolve to live honourably for their sakes who are gone before, 'to do justly, to love mercy, and to walk humbly with your God.' And it may be that, coming so, you too will be able to take a prophet's words upon your lips, and say, 'In the year that the King died, I saw the Lord.'

XXV

The Final Doxology

'Unto Him that loved us, and washed us from our sins
in His own blood, and hath made us kings and priests
unto God and His Father; to Him be glory and dominion for ever and ever. Amen.' — REV. i. 5, 6.

NORMAN MACLEOD OF THE BARONY OF GLASGOW, WHO WAS
the friend and confidant of Queen Victoria, once declared
that he could sum up everything that religion meant for him
in a single sentence. The sentence was this: 'There is a
Father in heaven who loves us, a brother Saviour who died
for us, a Spirit who helps us to be good, and a Home where
we shall all meet at last.' Truly a noble summary of a great
soul's creed!

Suppose that today you were asked to give your faith in a
sentence, could you do it? They once asked Denney that;
and his answer was — 'I believe in God through Jesus
Christ, His Only Son, our Lord and Saviour.' That, he said,
would cover everything. And again it was a noble answer.
Could you do it — put your whole gospel into a dozen
words? It is indeed a searching test; and every Christian, in
this age of the clash of rival doctrines and philosophies of
life, must feel acutely the challenge of the question to his
own soul.

You who stand as Christ's representatives tonight, thank
God if you can say that, amid much that is still dark and
mysterious and beyond your grasp, there are some things,
at least of which in His mercy He has made you dead sure,
surer than of life itself, some few, deep, simple things which

He has laid constrainingly upon heart and conscience with the command, 'There is your gospel; go out and herald that!'

And if you were to try to find a single sentence which would gather up into itself these central and decisive things by which you live, could any better words be fashioned than these of the seer of Revelation? 'Unto Him that loved us, and washed us from our sins in His own blood, and hath made us kings and priests unto God and His Father; to Him be glory and dominion for ever and ever. Amen.'

'*Unto Him that loved us.*' That is the foundation of everything. That is the rock-bottom of the universe. That is the conviction on which, like Browning's Festus, you can gamble with your soul. 'God, Thou art Love! I build my faith on that.'

I know there are other aspects of the gospel besides this. I know there is what St. Paul called 'the terror of the Lord'. I know there is what the writer to the Hebrews meant when he cried, 'Our God is a consuming fire.' I know that the sentimental religion which makes the righteous Father of Christ a mere principle of amiability and good-natured indulgence has no justification whatever, either in Scripture or in experience.

But I know also this — that any man who has once gazed into the eyes of Jesus is entitled to stand and cry to all the sons of men, even to the most sinful, shabby and wretched, 'God loves you! God is reconciled to you! Underneath you are God's everlasting arms.'

It is worth noticing that the Revised Version has turned the past tense into a present. 'Unto Him that loveth us.' is the true translation. Not only at Bethlehem where He shared our human lot; not only in Galilee, where He laid His hands on lepers' sores, and bound up the broken-hearted, and called the prodigals home; not only at Calvary, where

His love lighted a beacon blaze which a thousand ages cannot extinguish — but today, and tomorrow, and for ever, 'Unto Him that loveth us!' We know all the past tenses of the Christian religion — 'born of the Virgin Mary, suffered under Pontius Pilate, crucified, dead, and buried, the third day rose again from the dead' — we know all the past tenses: do we know the glorious present tenses of religion? Do we know the Christ who is out on the streets of the world to-night, seeking and finding the souls of men, the Christ who this very day has been drying the tears of the broken-hearted, and smoothing the pillow of the suffering, and driving out devils in the name of the Lord God Almighty — do we know Him? Unto Him that loveth us now — to Him whose love, though older than creation, is yet younger than this morning's dawn; to Him whose love is a perpetual unwearied intercession for our souls which will still be pleading for us on the very Day of Judgment; to Him who has your name written now across His heart, and will never in time or eternity let you go — to Him that loveth us be glory. That is the foundation of everything.

But now note the next thing. 'Unto Him that loveth us, *and loosed us from our sins by His blood.*' For you see, that is love in action. That is love's most characteristic action.

There is a kind of love which never gets into action at all. Heine has described how once he stood before the great statue of the Venus of Milo, now in the Louvre, and gazed on that matchless perfection of grace and dignity and beauty. 'But oh!' he cried, 'what was it worth? For she had no arms, the goddess, no hands to reach out and help poor beaten souls like me!' But God's love in Christ has arms strong enough to lift the universe, and hands — pierced hands — gentler than a mother's when she tends her child. God's love acts. 'He loved us,' says this man, 'and washed us from our sins.'

What else is all the world needing but just that? There is one stanza of Lucy Whitmell's *Christ in Flanders* that expresses it.

'Though we forgot You — You will not forget us —
We feel so sure that You will not forget us —
    But stay with us until this dream is past.
And so we ask for courage, strength, and pardon —
Especially, I think, we ask for pardon —
    And that You'll stand beside us to the last.'

There speaks the voice of man's deepest need in every age. 'Especially, I think, we ask for pardon.' And so the proclamation of the Church down the centuries has been, in the haunting words of the negro spiritual, 'free grace and dying love'. Is there anything else worth preaching?

When St. Augustine's end was near, and his strength was fast ebbing away, he begged one of his friends and disciples to paint on the wall opposite his bed the words of the thirty-second Psalm: 'Blessed is he whose transgression is forgiven, whose sin is covered. Blessed is the man unto whom the Lord imputeth not iniquity.' And the dying man lay there, gazing at the words, steadying his soul on them as the darkness gathered in — 'Blessed the man who is forgiven!' Will there be anything else worth clinging to at last? To Him that loves us — and has loosed us from our sins!

Does someone say, following the prevalent fashion, 'Sin? There is no such thing. Let us banish that stupid word from our vocabulary! Let us file its jagged edges away! Let us be finished with such antiquated notions' — does someone suggest that?

My friend, look at the world as it is today, and think again. Look at the international scene. If you do not like the word 'sin', don't use it, get some other word. I care not what you call it, nor what theories you have about its origin. The point is — the thing is there, tragically there, working against the living God — 'the universal insanity', as Seneca called it.

But indeed, we do not need to look at the world; we have only to look at our own hearts — for we are here (as Charles Kingsley used to say to his people in the village church at Eversley) 'to talk about what is really going on in your soul and mine.' And when we think of all the ways in which we have blundered, or take our life and compare the might-have-been with the actuality, or hear across the clamour of our God-forgetting days the still small voice of Jesus, or walk the fields of Galilee where first we learnt what love and truth and purity could mean, or sit in some quiet upper room with Christ and feel His eyes upon our soul — does that not dissipate once and for all the illusion that there is nothing to be forgiven? In our hearts, we know this thing called sin is fact. We know what it means to face strong, masterful temptations, and we know what it means to be beaten. We know what it means — God pity us — to settle down after a time in dull apathy, fettered by the shackles of habit, soiled and shabby and feckless and resigned. And we know what it means, thank God, sometimes to grow dissatisfied with all that, angry at our own commonplaceness, and to cry 'Oh God, to get out of all this, and to be free and strong and conquering and clean!'

Well, says the gospel, you can. 'Loved us, and loosed us from our sins.'

There was once in the city of Florence a massive, shapeless block of marble, which seemed fitted to be the raw material of some colossal statue. One sculptor after another tried his hand at it, without success. They cut and carved and hewed, till it seemed hopelessly disfigured. But then came Michelangelo's turn. He began by having a house built right over the block of marble, and for long months he was shut up there with it, and none knew what he was doing. But at last there came a day when he flung open the door and told them to come in; and they looked, and there before their eyes was — not now a shapeless, meaningless block — but the magnificent statue of David, one of the glories of the world. So Christ takes lives defeated and disfigured, and refashions them into the very image of God. 'To Him that loveth us — and loosed us from our sin.'

No measuring-line has ever been invented that can fix the limits of that grace. I put it to you tonight: have you ever seen the sinner yet whom God could not save? Search the Bible and the literature of the world. Can you find anywhere the words: 'I waited for the Lord, and He refused to hear my cry. I begged Him for His pardon, and He answered "No, we must draw the line somewhere — forgiveness is not for you" ' — can you find that anywhere? Turn to the Gospels. Do you remember the day when a poor creature came to Jesus, pathetic and broken and battered by the sins and sorrows of the years, crying, 'Jesus, Master, hear me and heal me,' and Jesus just shook His head sadly, and said, 'My friend, I am sorry for you, very sorry, and I'd love to help you, but even I am powerless here'? Do you remember that — in the Gospels? Of course you don't! For it is not there. Thank God it is not there. It never happened. What you do find there is a grace without end or limit — an evangel that could say to the man at Bethesda who had been for thirty-eight years incurable, 'Rise up and walk' — and to a poor wretch of a dying thief, on the very edge and rim of ruin, 'Friend, it is to be Paradise today'!

Do you say, 'Oh, but I have been defeated too often'? Then I say, Christ died for the defeated. Do you say, 'But don't you see? Life has beaten me so utterly'? I say, Christ died for the beaten. Do you say, 'Oh, but you don't understand! It is my character I am thinking of — it is fixed and hardened and bound and fettered as with chains'? I say, Christ died for the hardened. 'He brake the age-bound chains of hell.' To him that loved us, and loosed us from our sins by His blood — to Him be glory and dominion!

What next? When a man has been loved and loosed, what happens? 'Unto Him that *made us kings unto God.*' Do you catch the significance of that? It means that when a man knows he is loved, something happens to him. There is a new light in his eyes, and a new rhythm in his march, and a new dignity and poise and settled peace in his whole bearing. He has his head up to life now. He is walking on a redeemed earth with God. 'Thou hast made us kings,' cry the saints. 'I have a king's life with Christ,' exclaimed Samuel Rutherford. Have we got that in our religion?

There was a day when Jesus, passing down the thronged streets of Jericho, chose Zacchæus — of all unlikely people — to be His host for the night; and the crowd, watching them walking there together, grew fiercely critical and resentful. 'A strange prophet this,' they muttered, 'consorting with the riff-raff of the town! This finishes His reputation as far as we are concerned. Guest of Zacchæus!' Ah, but you should have seen Zacchæus in that hour, straightening himself up to his full total of inches, and flinging off the cringing serfdom of the years — the furtive, skulking look gone completely from his eyes, and a light upon his face that had never been there before. And why? Because one thought was beating in his brain and in his heart: 'Christ Jesus is not ashamed of me! He is glad to walk with me. He has even called me a "son of Abraham"!' And for the rest — what matter though the crowd were scoffing and vindictive? 'They say. What say they? Let them say!' The man lifted his head, and marched down the street like a king.

> 'All I could never be,
>   All, men ignored in me,
>   This, I was worth to God!'

He has made us kings.

Have we got that in our religion? The early Church had it. There was a second-century sceptic called Celsus who flung the vitriol of his sarcasm at the followers of the Nazarene. 'Just look at them,' he cried, 'poor, pathetic conglomeration of slaves and artisans and illiterates and gaol-birds and nonentities — the offscourings of the world!' Yes, Celsus, poor and pathetic indeed — and yet, sons of God, every man of them, brothers of the Christ; and therefore able to confront life with level eyes, and to stand before governors and rulers unashamed! He has made us kings.

There is a kind of modern religion which has lost that royal note completely. It is excessively apologetic. It does not proclaim, it ventures to suggest. It says, 'If you will allow me to say so, it is possible — it is just possible — that we may be sons of God.' Oh, for the apostolic spirit! If God be for us — God as Christ has revealed Him — who can be against us? If the everlasting Father believes in us, who has any power to hurt us? If Christ, knowing us exactly as we are, and everything that has ever happened in our life, can, and does most truly love us, who or what can daunt us? Son of man, stand upon thy feet, and lift high the banner of the Lord.

Now there is just one thing more in this great summary of religion by the seer of Revelation. 'Loved us — loosed us — made us kings — *and made us priests to God.*' That means direct access to God in prayer. It means that you, tonight, can look God full in the face for yourself. And that, too, is Jesus' gift.

Does someone say — 'Oh prayer! That is just the old advice — not much help in that, prayer does not get things done'? My friend, do you think that all the saints of all the ages have been fools? Was Christ, climbing to the mountain-top or kneeling in Gethsemane, deluded? Does the man who says there is no such thing as an answer to prayer know better than Jesus? Ah, how the praying Christ rebukes our prayer-lessness! 'Ye people,' cries the psalmist, 'pour out your heart before Him!'

Every soul, through Christ, has the right of access. In the old days it was different. High on the rock of Jerusalem stood the Temple; and in the Temple there was one barrier after another to keep men back from the shrine. 'No thoroughfare to God' was the rule, except for the high priest, who only once a year might enter. And before the holiest place of all there hung the veil, the great massive curtain of blue and scarlet and purple; and if any seeking soul had dared to lay a hand upon the veil, 'In the name of God, stand back!' would have been the cry, 'Back, man, for your life!' But one day Jesus died; and in the very moment of his death, says the evangelist, something happened in that Temple on the hill. There was a sudden loud rending sound. And the terrified priests ran in, and looked, and the veil was hanging torn from top to bottom, like a poor, worth-less rag — as though God Himself had said, 'Let them all come! Fling wide the gates of access, and let Me gather them home to My heart.' 'He hath made us' — and that means you and me — 'priests to God.'

Don't patch up that torn veil! Don't think there is need for someone to go knocking at heaven's back-doors when God's wandered sons come home! 'He arose, and came to his Father.' It is written on the title-deeds of Christianity in the very blood of Jesus, that that right of way is open. Don't let anything or any one hold you back! Even if your own sins try to hold you back, don't allow it. Be like John Newton, the hymn-writer:

> 'I may my fierce accuser face,
> And tell him Thou hast died.'

Fling that challenge at the sour, snarling faces of those sins
— 'Christ has died! Therefore, stand out of the way, you,
for God has bidden me come.'

> 'Just as I am — Thy love unknown
> Has broken every barrier down.'

He hath made us priests to God.

And so this man in Revelation sums it all up at last, and
gathers it into one great, glowing doxology. 'Unto Him who
has done all that — loved us and loosed us and made us
kings and priests — *unto Him be glory and dominion for
ever*.'

Here are we tonight, standing in the blood-bought
succession of the man who wrote these words, and sharing
the same great experience: are we giving Christ the glory?
'Ah, Mr. Spurgeon,' said an old woman whom the great
preacher was visiting, 'if Jesus Christ does save me, He shall
never hear the last of it!' Can we understand that? Do we,
like Charles Wesley, ever stand 'lost in wonder, love, and
praise'? Are we giving our Lord the glory?

'Unto Him,' cries the seer, 'be glory and dominion.' 'I see
a day coming,' he seems to say, 'when all the ends of the
earth will come crowding into Christ's allegiance. I see
Jesus, once despised and rejected, once savagely criticised
and hated with malignity, once crucified on the battlefields
of Europe, Africa, and Asia, I see Him coming up out of that
tribulation, and sitting on the throne of eternity. I hear the
song of the serried ranks of the redeemed, "Bring forth the
royal diadem, and crown Him Lord of all." Unto Him it is
coming — the glory and the dominion!'

Is that just a dream? A pious, pathetic hope? On the
contrary. It is sure as God Himself. The only question is,
Will you and I have a share in it when it comes?

Let us dedicate ourselves without delay to Christ the King. Every day of our life, let us renew and reaffirm the dedication. And then, when 'the evening comes, and the busy world is hushed, the fever of life is over, and our work done,' yonder in Immanuel's land we shall see Him face to face, the King in His beauty; and the cry of our adoring hearts will be, 'Blessed Jesus, Lord and Redeemer of men — the half was never told!'